Afterwords

by Lyle Crist

Mount Union College
Alliance, Ohio

AFTERWORDS
An English Prof's Reflections on a Campus Career

Copyright © 1989 by Lyle Crist

All rights reserved. This book may not be duplicated in any way without the expressed written consent of the publisher or author, except in the form of brief excerpts or quotations for the purposes of review. The information contained herein may not be duplicated in other books, databases or any other medium without the written consent of the publisher or author. Making copies of this book, or any portion for any purpose other than your own, is a violation of United States copyright laws.

ISBN: 0-9624800-0-2

Printed in the United States of America

Published by:
Mount Union College
Alliance, Ohio 44601
(216) 821-5320

Contents

1   Who? Me?
2   Surely Not I
3   Teaching as a Humbling Experience
4   Take the Stars With You
5   The Olde Prof
6   Relations with the Public
7   Bonehead Composition
8   Who Really Reads?
9   Encounters of the Campus Kind
10   Thinking
11   Newshawks -- and a Few Chickens
12   Traditions
13   Everybody's Doing It
14   Meet God
15   English and the Technical World?
16   It Never Ends

I am grateful to Mount Union College for many things.

In some way perhaps these reflections will show even in small degree the appreciation I have for my colleagues through the years, for the administration, and most of all for the young people who came into my many classes.

We had fun. And we had learning. Certainly I learned from them... valuable, honest, reflections which I cherish.

There are some anecdotes which follow that might suggest a kind of "looking down" on these young people. Maybe I did on occasion, but in these reflections I do not want to detract in any way from their own personalities, their own achievements, and their own perspectives.

The years have been rewarding with insight, interaction, and awareness. I hope that in some degree these pages will be entertaining to read and, more importantly, effective in sharing those insights, those interactions, and those awarenesses.

We never stop learning!

1
Who? Me?

You're supposed to roam around the classroom sniffing out mistakes, anything that the Queen's English doesn't accept. You're supposed to be hard nosed in catching all the improprieties -- the dangling participle, the indefinite pronoun. And whatever you do, be sophisticated -- preferably keep your nose in the air, wave a stick, scribble on the blackboard, use deep intonations as you produce formal, dispirited harangues (called "lectures") on grammar, linguistics, rhetoric, and obscure writers of the eighteenth century.

Stress parts of speech. Always stress parts of speech.

And drill work. See the words. This is a noun. A noun is a doer and a verb is a doee (or is it the doing?); memorize the terms and don't worry about the big picture.

They've been memorizing all their high school years and nothing has registered to this point.

Keep hoping. And drilling.

There is the tale of the English professor who was out to get the kid in the back row -- the perennial dum-dum who had trouble spelling his middle name and knew not his home address ("down the street that way, you know?"); the prof, knowing it was solid humiliation coming up, enjoyed the opportunity. He was determined that the rest of the class should be aware how inferior this one was.

"Name two personal pronouns," the prof smirked.

The kid stared in awe. Then he blurted, "Who? Me?"

The prof had to give him an "A."

So much for parts of speech. Wear brown, with some tatters. Be sober (in class). Be harsh with grades. Most of all, have a dozen idiosyncrasies -- those special, strange mannerisms which will distinguish you as a member of the academy. Something like never tying your shoelaces, or wearing an outdated necktie, or having a leaky ballpoint.

Always be late for class, forget occasionally where it is held, use a scholarly lecture on *Paradise Lost* by mistake in a beginning composition class.

Stare at the girls. From time to time you might possibly pat the girls on the shoulder as they go by; certainly invite them to the office for pseudo-conferences, and give the basketball players high grades for other reasons -- something in proportion to their height.

Go around carrying some heavy tome -- perhaps a two-volume set exploring linguistics, titled *Etymological Implications of the Anglo-Saxon Pre-Determinism of the 16th Century*.

Frequent the library, of course, dawdling over current issues of the English Journal, The Journal of the Modern Language Association, and the Science Fiction Quarterly. If you do not approve of the last, you may substitute the Flying Saucer Annual or other similar publication.

Let your browns be tweeds. Something British. With a few patches, not necessarily for current style. Ride a bicycle, preferably an old model with rusting chrome. Wheel it along the campus sidewalks, weaving through bands of students. Offer them a cheery "hail!" or a hearty "cheerio!".

Have a definite idiosyncrasy with regard to study habits. Imitate Albert Einstein, who, they say, walked along the curbs at Princeton with one foot on the street, the other on the curb -- so that he could read while walking, not needing to glance up from his book to check his direction.

Smoke a pipe. This helps, on most occasions, to give an appropriate "prof" image. Old pipe, with crusted saliva. Have tobacco pouches bulging in coat pockets, forever wrinkling the coat which is never pressed anyway from football season to the holidays. Use an off brand of tobacco, something formulated in Ireland or Portugal.

Have a beard, of course. A gentle mixture of sandy (or red) hair with wisps of gray. Gray can dominate as well, but there should be, in that instance, wisps of sandy (or red) hair. Balding perhaps. But flowing. Wear a tam, bowler, or a sandy (or red) stocking cap, sometimes forgetting to remove the topper while you are lecturing to a literature class.

Background is important. Debate team in high school, editor of "The Raider" school paper, then to the university with a fraternity affiliation, English major (emphasis on Renaissance literature, a minor in modern poetry). The school could be Illinois or Harvard or the University of Washington or (possibly) North Carolina State. Edit the literary magazine and see that several radical articles against U.S. intervention in foreign affairs creep into the otherwise staid publication. Have a graduate degree, of course -- two or three, in fact. A master's at Northwestern in 18th century English literature, thesis on Robert Browning's dog's influence on Browning's life and literature. Then to the University of California or Columbia or (possibly) North Carolina State for a Ph.D. in contemporary comparative literature.

Have three papers published during your graduate work in the scholarly quarterlies, including the *Journal of Browning's Dog's Influence*. Have at least one published article exploring (in great detail) the obscenity of Allen Ginsberg and his poetry. Early teaching done at Missoula College in Backhand, Missouri. Of course, some teaching along with the graduate work at Northwestern or Columbia or (possibly) North Carolina State. Freshman writing courses -- a full load of them at Missoula College where the football team loses seven games each season.

Several book reviews in the *Dullard's Quarterly* (circulation 600) after three years of losing seasons at Missoula, then on to West Virginia Wesleyan or San Jose State and a chance to teach two courses in Renaissance poetry, then on up the academic ladder until today, in your "later years," at Brown or Concordia or Iowa State or Michigan we have the beard, pipe, tweeds, bicycle -- and security.

Be terribly liberal in politics. Snort at the thought of injecting the topic of morality into the teaching of writing.

The English prof.

Who? Me?

2
Surely Not I

English prof. Small, midwestern, church-related liberal arts college. People want to know more about the classroom at Mount Union College in Ohio. "How many students do you have, Prof. Crist?"

"About one out of ten."

No, it isn't really that bad, of course. If that ratio held up, if I detested the work, I should leave immediately to try deep sea fishing or hang gliding. Those enrolled are young people who, for the most part, want to get their money's worth from my classes. Many are bewildered about society, about money, about careers, about themselves. Some bring on most of the bewilderment through their own actions, but most are passive. College plays a part in all of this. My affiliation with Mount Union College in northeastern Ohio began some 36 years ago; the span of years has continually revealed the range and diversity of human talent and motivation. Perhaps I could find out as much about humanity in a different profession -- but that is for others to attest.

I taught at Purdue University, at Indiana University, and at Iowa State College prior to Mount Union. My field is communications-- literature and writing. Why study writing at all in an era of telecommunications, instant voice and picture? We write for one reason: we have something we want to share. And the most visible, lasting, and efficient form for that sharing is words on paper. Not all may agree. In the mid-nineteenth century Henry David Thoreau did not

not wish to speak to one Ellen Sewell of his deep love for her. "Love that must be spoken is not love at all," he is said to have told a friend.

Perhaps. But the fact that Ellen turned down Henry's idealized love is an indication that some further communication was probably in order.

Ralph Ellison, speaking at a conference for teachers of creative writing, put his finger on the value of writing when he said, "Language inspirits lives with values ... language resonates." The resonating, echoing, reminding aspect of writing -- that's why we need to write effectively. Somebody else reads it. Someone else can reflect upon our words, can come in a degree to the full perception of what it is in our minds.

Writing is an afterthought.

The very worst phrase in the English language is neither profane nor obscene. It is a worn-out classic of lazy expression, the one you use and I use and all my students use -- and the one which ought to be placed with atomic wastes at the bottom of the sea. It's the one which goes, "You know what I mean?"

You know? Know what I mean?

I get a chance to talk to an Olympic high diver, the kind I watch on the ABC "Wide World of Sports," the fellow who dives from a hundred feet into a little pool in Miami Beach as the Goodyear blimp photographs from overhead. The fellow who goes contorting downward in awesome twists and turns and loops, knife-edging into the water in perfect form. I have to hold my nose when I fall in from poolside. I ask this fellow, "What goes through your mind just before those awesome leaps? What does it feel like to be up there?"

"Well, you get up there -- you know what I mean?"

"No. Not really." I've never been up there.

"You feel the wind and you look down and you get this feeling -- you know what I mean? This feeling, you know, and you really have it, you know what I mean?"

I have two options. I can be honest and forthright: "No, you dum-dum. That's why I asked the question!"

Or I cop out, saying, "Uh huh."

That's the path we usually take. Grunts and groans and simplest sounds. Animals make basic sounds, so why not just get along with the grunts, the uh huhs?

Because we are human beings. Not animals. And a graduate of Mount Union College made the point so well. "A parakeet has keener sight than man. A dog has sharper hearing. A mink has a better sense of smell. Yet a man puts the parakeet in a cage, chains the dog in a kennel, and drapes the mink over his wife's shoulders. Why?"

He answered his own question. "Because man has a better mind...he can imagine solutions, invent tools, communicate ideas through language, and accumulate knowledge through written records..."

Women and men -- humanhood -- have the potential to articulate, to use some 600,000 different words rather than a few grunts. And that's the primary reason why we have English profs around.

And this is why we teach writing in college. There is no communication when the speaker or writer says "You know what I mean?" There is communication only when the listener or the reader can say, "Hey! Now I know what you mean!" Not until then.

Until then there is no inspiriting of values. No resonating. No echoing. No sharing. Perhaps "resonating" and "inspiriting" are too flowery for some. What else do we have? I taught American literature with echoes following me wherever I was on campus. More than echoes -- it is Walt Whitman and Ellen Glasgow and Mark Twain and Saul Bellow. Writing is always people. Always humanity.

Names of students will fade from my thought, time's watershed curls the directory pages. But my classes are always people as well. Not names, not rules, not texts. Some students came from wealthy homes, with lives full of idle hours on campus, unsure; those from less wealth work extra hours for the food service, for the secretarial pools, for maintenance projects. Many struggle to meet the private college tuition which may be two or three times that of dozens of community colleges and branches of Ohio State and Kent State which surround us.

And some have questions. Nearly 30 years ago Judy Gordon raised a question in her writer's journal for one of my classes: "If this is supposed to be a Methodist school, then why do we have to eat fish every Friday night?"

And some make novel observations. This from another student: "The rich eat just like the poor. I served in the President's dining room today and as I was pouring coffee for a Hart Shafner and Marx gentleman he catapulted a piece of potato from his fork through a one-and-a-half gainer, neatly onto his lap..."

Students and words themselves have much in common; some words have long lives, change little in meaning and use; others are flexible, dynamic, finding relationship with changing times. Meanings and values alter with both young people and language.

Many who sign up for my creative writing course see themselves as celebrity writers, earning huge incomes for their golden words.

"How can I get published?"

They've read 195 articles about Michael Jackson and rightfully conclude that they, too, can write well enough to publish -- publish almost anything. My answer has been a remarkably efficient one: "Write a letter to the editor of your hometown newspaper and we'll see how well you communicate." The pay is nothing, but the satisfaction of seeing your very own words in print -- and, what's more, knowing that thousands may be reading those golden words -- is significant.

Most consider this form of publication too low for them, yet they could benefit from at least reading such letters. It takes sweat and nerve to sit down and express some deep-felt emotion. The cost of postage, too. Give letters-to-the-editor writers credit for trying to do something.

Even if it does not always turn out as planned. I have shared with my classes this well-intended letter from an Ohio newspaper:

> Dear Editor:
> I want to express my appreciation to all the kind neighbors who assisted my recent illness...

(We can see those neighbors, crowding around the bed, shouting nasty things, turning off the heat, throwing stones at the poor, ill one, taking away the bed pan.)

> In a world in which so many people do not think about caring for their neighbors, it is good to know there are some in this area willing to help. My hope now is that one of these neighbors will have a serious illness, too, so that I can show my gratitude in return.

Good heavens! Is that what the writer really meant? Of course not. Her words did not do justice to her emotion.

However, she did try -- and that's important. No congratulations, however, on the command of language. I'd say the grade is "F."

Maybe this is why we have English classes in college; to help people write better letters to the editor. Maybe we could form a national association, a self-help agency. Many apparently need it. Consider this opening to a letter addressed to a California paper; it incorporates what I'd call a "rambling pronoun" -- in this case, the word "this:"

> Dear Editor:
> I work in a liquor store. We have been held up four times. Unfortunately, this is the only means I have of making a living...

Which is the "only means?" How will we ever know?

Everybody has feelings, fears, opinions. It's tragic when we don't succeed in conveying them effectively. In the spring of 1970 Mount Union College went through a controversial experience, fed by a small group of disgruntled white students who fomented a series of trumped-up events including two cross burnings. The plan was to stir up black students and lay siege against the conservative white students.

Kent State University with its own tragic problems was just a half-hour from us, and the overall atmosphere that spring spurred much concern. Black students, grieved and unaware of the fraudulent nature of the burning, rightly accosted others with complaints. On a given day they took over classes at Chapman Hall. Two approached me as I entered my American lit classroom. "We want to take over today... talk about the issues, you know?"

"Good. We aren't getting anything else done. Let's clear the air and explain things."

I was eager to cooperate. Besides, they were both considerably more hefty than I.

They were also eager. Motivated. Emotionally high. And they blew their chance.

Time after time in responding to questions (most of them from the conservative white students of fraternity status) the two who took over the class did not do justice to their feelings.

"Well, it's like, you know, man, like this ain't right, you know what I mean?"

I have no objection to the use of "ain't" in this case. That was, in fact, the very least of any concerns I had.

What was terribly wrong was their unfortunate cop-out, their leaning back and using the laziest phrase of all.

Then a direct question: "What's so bad about burning a cross?"

"Well, you know, like it is degrading. It really gets to you, you know?"

I was sitting in the back row, my head moving like the pendulum on a kitchen clock. "No! No! No! The class does not know what it means. Tell them!" All they got was a series of generalities and cop-outs and everybody shrugged and everybody left to throw their frisbees and play tennis and turn up their stereos and I sat there wondering if I would ever get anybody to think -- and to express. We had been studying colonial literature in that class; I mused what would have happened if Thomas Paine had written, "These are the times that, like, you know, really get to us -- you know what I mean?"

What if Abraham Lincoln had said, "We are engaged in a really big thing, you know? Testing whether, like, we can hang in, you know?..."

There is nothing we cannot explain in suitable degree through language. It takes thought and effort, of course.

Walt Whitman put it this way: "The English language befriends the grand American expression. It is brawny enough and limber enough and full enough..."

What's the purpose of an English prof? Among problems all around us -- racial, social, economic -- an English prof's job is not to see that all people think alike. I have my own set of values -- and they differ considerably from those I read of in the *National Enquirer* (or even the campus paper, the *Dynamo*, on occasion); but my role in being a prof is not primarily to have my students think as I do. It is, however, to have my students do justice in expressing their own thinking. You and I may not agree on our points of view about anything. But, doggonit, we ought to be able to understand what our disagreements are.

Times change. And so does language -- and the sciences.

Chemists keep discovering new elements. When I took undergraduate chemistry I think the figure was 92; now I am told it is 107 or 108, with more offstage. Illinium was unearthed at the University of Illinois, Polenium in Poland ... we should anticipate Mount Unonium one of these days!

But the small size of Mount Union sometimes turns away my fellow professors at academic meetings. They mutter things behind my back. No Nobel winners, no cyclotrons, no riverboat theater, no national writers' conferences -- not even 10,000 in attendance at football games (more like 1,500). Size is equated with significance, as though Einstein directed a laboratory of 400 graduate assistants, or that the best poets had a 50,000-seat stadium for their readings. As a matter of fact, Einstein did have a laboratory -- the universe. But he had few assistants, and I understand his office frequently consisted of a pad of paper inside his coat pocket.

Yet the academic process goes on, and the small college label loses some, if not all, of its negative connotation -- because the sources are the same. I found out some years ago that the English literature text being used at Mount Union was the same as that adopted for similar courses at Harvard. Not as much ivy around the dust jacket, though.

The scholarly mystique is much the same, too. East or west, we're all a bit absent-minded; I've spent the better part of my lunch hour time trying to figure out where I parked the car. On occasion, I've remembered in time that my wife Marilyn was using it. On one occasion I spent twenty minutes looking for my bicycle before remembering I had walked that morning.

I can seldom remember to take my magnetic-ink character-recognition check book with special deposit slip and magic personalized number with me when I clutch my paycheck tightly in one hand and hurry to the bank. "Do you have your magnetic-ink character-recognition personalized deposit slip with your personal number with you?" The clerk yawns as she asks.

"I forgot. I was reviewing Faulkner's work at the University of Virginia and his answers regarding his short novel *The Bear* on my way down. I'm giving a pop quiz this afternoon." I am cheerful at this point.

"Can't accept the money without the magnetic-ink character." I put down Faulkner and plead. Conference ensues and, although the check is finally deposited, I am given a stern warning that the complex IBM machines may short circuit if I am so absent-minded again. Should I cause $65,000 worth of electronic damage just because of something William Faulkner once said?

No. But I'd be pleased with the smallest share of that money for classroom accessories. Walk into any English classroom and you'll discover the lack of sophistication. Barren yellow cinder block walls, timeless catalog furniture. I'd like carpeting, decorator colors, original paintings, softer lights -- but all I really need is a chair and a student. In fact, the chair can be eliminated.

At Mount Union College the oldest building is the center for classes in English -- and other humanities. Chapman Hall; Old Main. Civil War era and a remodeling in the 1960s.

Enter with me through crowded corridors under fluorescent panels, down cold terrazzo floors once wooden and warm and squeaky, now sterile. Forget the laboratory equipment, the spectrometers, the Wilson Cloud chambers. Walk into room 109 where in bygone days the walls were dark brown and yellow on a chipped plaster wall. Fluted columns once interrupted staid rows of desks; now the ceilings are stressed for the upper three floors and I can scan the room without distraction, except for the front-row coeds who cast probing, yet oblique glances.

The desk is without adornment for the prof. I perch on top, leg draped in casual fashion for a suspended moment, then comment. "We'll be involved with diverse topics; we'll read more widely in this class than in any other -- and we should be thinking deeply, too. If we do our job you'll do more thinking than you've ever done before -- for any class."

Impossible goal for a freshman writing class, dedicated to nouns and pronouns? No, it's a legitimate goal. There are times, though, when I get nowhere.

I lean against the brownboard (which used to be black, but brown shows an updating of decor); I get chalkdust all over my blue sportcoat. After a while, it is difficult to determine which is chalkdust and which is dandruff.

"Let's consider the books you've discussed in high school. Write a paper of 300 words in which you tell me something of the books that have meant the most to you. Title this paper 'Books Discussed in High School.' "

That evening I'm glancing over the papers, grading two or three, getting the idea of the preparation, the vocabulary and basic writing skills. Then I leave my study, flip TV buttons, return in new spirits. I pick up Richard's paper on books discussed in high school.

He has written at the top of the first page, "Books Disgusted in High School." He may have meant it that way. The paper gets worse. He notes, "Surely the book I enjoyed reading the most was an autobiography of Alaska." Naturally. Alaska always was a fine writer!

September leaves turn to gold, the gridiron team struggles, the papers keep coming in. I ask students to write about their families, something of their backgrounds. We are getting to know, to appreciate, each other. At home, mid the flamboyant leaves I have not yet raked, I stare at the papers. Peter writes of his ancestry: "My father was a minister's son until he was seven." I trust that Peter's grandfather changed jobs when Peter's father was seven. If not, the *National Enquirer* should know about this.

12

Looking to the future -- when the leaves are gone, when we have finished weeping over their loss, when we applaud the accumulation both of snow and of freshman themes, I have the class write of their aspirations. I am an old fuddy-duddy, mind you, and I may have missed the mark on this one, but I ponder whether Dave really meant it this way: "My highest hope is that I will marry the right women."

Perhaps all men have dreamed of this, but I must ponder my philosophy books. Did David misspell or was it a problem in vocabulary? Or is there no problem at all? I gave him a B minus. For dreaming. I have been caught dreaming. And I have caught the *Dynamo*, the campus weekly, napping, too. "The coach will use two tight ends in the game tomorrow..." Ah! And we're a church-related college, too!

I must admit, though, the players do weave around a bit on the field at times. However, I'm no authority. I'm not the world's greatest sports fan -- having had my fill of prima donna athletes in the professional world who make more money in two weeks than I do in five years and then expect me to willingly pay $25 to see them complain to the referee or umpire. In addition, professional athletes figure in my scheme for the single step which would, in one moment, uplift the quality of our language a hundredfold: stop interviewing professional athletes on television. I mean, like, you know, like, we gotta go out there and, you know, really play -- you know what I mean?

Oh, well, now it's the old prof who's dreaming. A typographical error last season did, however, give me a basis for our losing season on the amateur level. Skipping lightly through the six pages of the campus weekly I found out that, for tomorrow's game, Randy Shultz will be "playing right tickle."

Always wondered what they did down there on the line of scrimmage!

After making what probably were a few critical remarks about the team one October afternoon, I had a paper of defense from one of the freshman members of our vaunted gridiron team. Pointing out the skills and talents required for all team members, he wrote, "After all, it takes a lot of talent to center a football fifteen yards between your legs."

I was impressed. I wrote in the margin, "Does Guinness know about this?" I figured my freshman had the biggest spread on campus.

Our language moves in fascinating ways. And here is a freshman girl getting so close to the right word -- but not enough. She wrote,

"My aunt died without coming out of a comma." Well, that probably wasn't as painful as being in a semi-colon.

Or as painful as being an English prof!

We were checking credentials, weren't we? Let's see how I fit. I have the beard. It's white now, greater accumulation of hair on my chin than on the top of my head. And I cherish the anonymous postcard delivered to me in 1971 when the beard was new.

"Mt. Union College professors who are too lazy to shave and too stingy to get a hair-cut are just as offensive to the people as the rest of the hairy animals that now roam the campus. It is a disgusting sight!"

Dick Button, a senior then, saw the card and told me I'd better "heed this warning from the citizenry...the pinkos are everywhere!"

We laugh about it now; Dick became a trustee of Mount Union. And I became the prof at the end of his career -- checking to see if I might yet fit. Agreed: sniffing out mistakes, looking at the girls' knees, having a beard, and having trouble telling who's awake and who's asleep.

Disagreed: tweed suits (knits are much better); harsh grades (I'm a softy); carrying heavy tomes around (I seldom get beyond the daily newspapers); the pipe (I never have smoked); debate team (I was too scared to give an oral report in high school); liberalism (I am a liberal -- but not in the conventional ways); undergraduate and graduate pedigree (well, let's get this out in the open: my undergraduate degree is from Purdue in aeronautical engineering and my graduate work stopped after a master's from Indiana University -- in journalism).

On balance, I didn't quite make the grade. If there are some heads in the back of the room bobbing back and forth like the pendulum on the kitchen clock, I will understand. Yet this melange of background produces the English prof.

Like, baby, we have come to this point because WE are really here. You know what I mean?

3

Teaching as a Humbling Experience

It is Monday morning. September 1972. Young men and women new to campus said farewells to parents, assorted kinfolk and a few beagles five days before. There followed intensive sessions with dorm leaders, food service personnel, the deans, faculty advisors and hosts of peers who said, "Don't believe any of that gump." All of this under the heading of Freshman Orientation. The Sunday chapel service attracted 60 percent of the incoming freshmen. The campus chaplain gave insights on campus and Christianity; following this was a cookout adjacent to the campus center -- which attracted 90 percent of the incoming freshmen. Times of friendships, renewals, and the great anticipation of attendance at their very first college classes.

The bookstore is crowded this Monday inasmuch as all have waited till the last minute to purchase texts -- heavy, multi-colored books which sold for $5 in the 1960s and for $25 and $35 in the 1980s, written usually by big-campus professors who retire on their earnings from 10,000-member freshman classes. The T-squares, felt-tip pens, assorted notebooks (with campus crest on cover), and stationery are all stuffed into totes and off students scurry to Chapman Hall.

Class begins at 10:10. Period III. I have chatted with colleagues about the Cleveland Indians, about white-water rafting, and about felt tip pens -- and now stride down the basement corridor to a yellow cinder block room in which the fate of nineteen freshmen is sealed. The eyeballing is mutual.

It is something akin to checking out a blind date, with no goodies in store for either one. I am wearing my wrinkled sportcoat, patch pockets, and wide necktie which is always three years off the pace of *Esquire* magazine. I carry a dictionary, three textbooks, a green gradebook, and a computer readout of names in English Composition, period III, fall term, code 789.

The class is all·set. They've been there waiting for me. I think of something Emerson said about going to church. I try to brush it away, but it keeps inching its way into my thought : "The best part of a church service," Emerson noted, "is the quietness before the sermon starts."

Surely that does not apply to my services.

"This is it." My voice is stentorian. "My young friends, the orientation period is over. Now it's down to business."

I draw the leg over edge of desk, smooth my pants in deliberate, slow movements as we all study the creases. Then I release the books and computer readout; I clear my throat. Thirty-eight eyes shift in cadence. "We're in for hard work in this class. Nine papers, a research project, grammar review, analysis of some of the good writers of today. The text is a demanding one and the assignments won't leave you much time for fooling around." It is like the day of doom and I am the voice in the sky. Their eyes are intent. Unbelieving, but intent.

I notice graffiti on the T-shirts. One young man displays a shirt stating simply, "Bull Shirt." A young lady next to him has full phrasing emblazoned across her bosom: "And every inch of me a woman." I offer no argument, but continue.

"You have had twelve years of schooling. Grade, junior high, high school -- now the big four at the top. You've had English in some form each year. I expect you to know how to spell, punctuate, write a decent paragraph, and make a point." For some reason I glance again at the young lady who is every inch a woman. I return reluctantly to my exhortation.

"OK, so you know all of these. It's our job now to go beyond them. We'll elevate the discussion. Tone and Style. The nuances of expression. It takes sweat and I'm going to get that out of you."

It is halftime at the Super Bowl and I am the best coach in the league. "We have a tough game ahead, but if you cooperate, if you're willing to work in this class, I promise you I'll be fair and you'll get your tuition's worth. We'll have assignments every day regarding your writing." I shift legs now and see another T shirt adage: "Exam is a four-letter word." I ignore it now and mention the texts, pointing out that the basic rhetoric is a book -- proudly held aloft -- titled *Man*

Expressed and that it is written by some old codger named Crist. "The best book of its kind," I add graciously. I am concerned now, however, due to the lack of knowing smiles, that some in the class will assume the author's name is Codger.

"We'll have tests every third week. We'll get into nouns and pronouns if we have to, but let's hope we can discuss the more literary aspects of writing."

It is silent. Somewhere I sense the muted weeping of a student who realizes this college and this campus and this professor of English are top-notch in their demands. I can almost forget all the books disgusted in high school, all of those who died without coming out of a comma. This class will be different!

"We'll meet a full 60 minutes each day. On time. The first assignment is in *Man Expressed*, four exercises on page 13. One side of the page, please, and in ink. I guess that just about takes care of the basics for now." I unwrap the leg, fondle the turquoise tie clip which I hope everyone has noticed, and ask if there are any questions.

A young man in the third row, wearing a shirt which merely says "Graffiti," raises a hand without hesitation.

I nod. I urge him to press his inquiry.

He does. "Who are you?"

I have neglected to inform them of my name. I will probably forget where I parked the car, too. I recover quickly, though, and say, "I wondered if anyone would ask that. You need to be alert, asking questions--all of you. I was testing you on that."

I go to the board and write my name. "Please note that the name 'Crist' does not have an 'h' in it. That is important. I am a full professor of English and Journalism. My office number is 343." I am writing this on the brownboard.

Then an afterthought. "Office hours will be posted on the door. You'll always find me there at the stated times if I can be of any other assistance."

"Any other questions?"

Another hand. "Yeah -- I thought this was a class in history."

A third hand goes skyward. "It says on the door to wait ten or fifteen minutes. Something about Prof. Saffell being late for class."

Other hands join in the maneuvers. Everyone nods. I am now concerned that perhaps there is the possibility that I have somehow gotten into the wrong room.

"Yes, well, I wanted to make sure you were in." I look at the class list furnished by the registrar. "Anybody here by the name of

Abramson? Ditherby? Smith?" The sky is darkening about me. "Fenster? McMichael?" I pick up my books and head for the doorway. "I just wanted to be helpful." I smile. I look at the creases in my pants. "I'm sure Prof. Saffell will be with you shortly." Another hand now. Well, I can retrieve some dignity by answering directly. I am pausing at the door. "Yes, young man. What is your question?"

"It's about that book you mentioned. The one by Codger. I heard it ain't really a very good one at all."

In the hallway I mutter things to myself about my career. It *is* a humbling experience, this academic groove.

I know very well these things would never happen to an aeronautical engineer. But they might happen to a professor of, say, mathematics. The story is told of an incredible experience of the noted Prof. David Hilbert in Germany many years ago. In the words of scientist Theodore van Karmon, Hilbert "at times fitted the type of German absentminded professor caricatured in American movies." One can understand that when one thinks about Hilbert at home, hosting a dinner party. His wife remarked to him that he was wearing an impossible tie. He promptly went upstairs to change it -- and failed to return. Nearly an hour went by before Mrs. Hilbert got upstairs to see what had happened. She found him in bed, fast asleep. According to van Karman, "He had started to change his tie, and since this was the normal way in which he started to undress for bed, he simply continued undressing and went to sleep, completely forgetting the dinner and his guests."

Now, that is a goal I might strive for, but which I do not believe I can attain. But I can, indeed, have humbling experiences back in the classroom -- even when I'm in the right classroom.

Consider an afternoon in 1977. I was in rare form that day, letting loose a stirring lecture on the achievements of Ben Franklin. We had finished the Puritan writers in American literature class, gone from William Bradford to Anne Bradstreet to Jonathan Edwards to a session on the trial of John Peter Zenger (he had called the governor a mad dog and that wasn't very nice but his acquittal was a landmark in our tradition of free expression). Now it was a turn to the age of reason and its illustrious Mr. Franklin.

I gave everything in the lecture: Franklin the printer, Franklin the philosopher, Franklin the diplomat, Franklin the autobiographer, traveller, scientist. Franklin the inspiration.

The class of 36 scribbled notes, listened, chuckled at the right times. I was moved. We had made progress. "Thus it was with Franklin, the truly significant author of diverse and noble achievement. His life -- a model of accomplishment for all of us to appreciate." I slumped against the brownboard, felt the chalkdust seeping through my clothes, but basked in the awareness of my own achievement.

Then Phil Stanga raised his hand.

"Yes, Phil; do you have a question?"

I had stirred him. The thrill of academic involvement and discovery! "Yeah. I have a question about this guy Franklin."

"Good."

Interaction.

"And what is it?"

"Yeah. Didn't he do a lot of messin' around, too?"

Caught again. The thrill now gone. As a matter of fact, Franklin did move around in amorous circles, but that wasn't to be the thrust of my inspiring lecture. There is also the tale of the student who, writing of Franklin's far-flung life, said that "Franklin moved to Philadelphia, got married, and discovered electricity." Probably the true sequence.

Humbling, this teaching profession. You're supposed to be the authority, knowing all the answers; when the prof makes a mistake in any form there is no one smaller in stature than that prof. I walk right into so many situations of my own undoing! One afternoon in freshman English class I noticed a halfback in a distant row talking throughout my lecture to a young lady. There was no contest; she was much more appealing than my lecture. Still, it was the professor's duty to be in charge and so I plunged into a confrontation designed to restore my leadership.

"Are you the professor in this class?" I had considerable authority in my voice.

The young man admitted that he was not the professor.

I said, "Then stop talking like an idiot!"

The class was dismissed shortly afterwards.

Whenever I get a bit too stuffy about my importance on campus (an event which occurs about once every decade) I am reminded of the classic results of a study done at Wayne State for the American Psychological Association regarding classroom modes of thought. "At any given instant in the college lecture hall," the report concluded, "20 percent of both men and women are thinking about sex, and only about 20 percent are paying attention to the professor."

I am presuming it is not the same 20 percent in those cases. Well, if my stirring lectures can keep pace with the fantasies and longing of my students, perhaps I am about as accomplished as I should hope for. The humility aspect of teaching began immediately for me. Graduate school had just been completed in 1947 and, for some strange reason, I had turned down a job in New York City, opting instead for teaching at Iowa State. New York did not appeal inasmuch as no housing was available for my young bride at that time -- and I had little intention of relocating without her. After all, she owned the new black Ford two-door and new cars were hard to get in the years following World War II, waiting lists as long as the exhaust on my 1938 Plymouth. It took more than exhaust to get to Ames, Iowa, however. Route 6 boasted curbs, if you please, along a hundred miles of rural roadway. I was glad the Ford was a relatively narrow car.

Anyway, comfortably settled there in a basement room three blocks from the Iowa State campus (with Marilyn doing wonders with the furnished hotplate), I began teaching Freshman English and technical writing in Beardshear Hall. Early that fall a competency exam was scheduled for all seniors at the College. Now, a writing competency test, terribly important, nonetheless is something no decent long-time faculty member desires to become involved with. First of all, it's given on a Saturday when all full professors should be enjoying the previous Sunday's *New York Times* (it took five days for it to reach Ames back then); also there were always the fresh young instructors who were anxious to make their marks.

They told me I fell into such a category. Actually, I had no choice. "You are assigned to proctor the senior writing competency test Saturday morning," the note read. "Report at 8: 30 a.m. along with..." I reported, little knowing that I was about to become the object of considerable concern.

"All right, you seniors," I announced. "You have two hours to develop this important paper. Now we will be watching for all your competency -- making sure you can spell, can punctuate, can write decent sentences, can use effective vocabulary and all that. If you can't spell, you will not be allowed to graduate in the spring unless you take a special course. Is that clear?"

Nods. Nervous fingers fondled pens and the seniors got set. "All right, I'll put the topic on the board now. Then you'll have two hours to respond. And no dumb mistakes!"

Picking up the chalk, I strode to the board. I wrote -- with as professional a scrawl as I could muster -- the topic which my elders had selected.

I wrote, "Attack or Defend the American Policy Towards Germany."

The motion at first went by me. They were all, of course, nervous. I simply said, "There it is," glancing at the board. "Now get to work. And remember -- no dumb mistakes. "

I began to stride up the side of the room, making the initial professional proctoring glances expected of me, unaware of the swelling movement and ultimate laughter in the lecture hall.

Finally one young man pointed out the problem. "You get graded, too?" he asked.

I have never used the word "policy" in a theme topic since that time.

The awkward situations never end. When I first affiliated with Mount Union, the college had regulations governing the use of alcohol. I rather liked the overall impact of what was, for many others, a strict approach. Now, due to student pressure and what I presume is a significant shift in the judgment of the Methodist Church which supports the college, alcohol is openly consumed on the campus. I observed a young man recently putting up a poster announcing a "SAE Keggar" for Saturday night. Another booze blast. Everybody come and get tanked. I took my case directly to the young man and growled as I passed by, "What did the SAEs ever do to help the world?"

Without hesitation: "Raised $55 for the multiple sclerosis fund last weekend." He put another thumbtack on the board. I hurried to the elevator. My growl had betrayed something much less than an intellectual exercise. And the student had won his case. I did, however, have opportunity to point out the misspelling of "kegger."

Not all profs growl -- but all have idiosyncrasies. I recall one back at Purdue who always stomped his right foot three times after putting an engineering problem on the board, then asking, "Now what do we do?" Kurt Vonnegut has a character in *Cat's Cradle* who always grabs his own buttocks, saying "Yes, yes, yes" in times of stress. There may be a relationship here. Doc Miller of the chemistry department at Purdue always stored a lump of coal under the demonstration table; whenever a student got too noisy (or talked to the girl next to him), Miller would ask the young man to come forward, hold out his hands.

Then Miller would place the lump of coal in them. "Hold this for me, please, till the end of the period."

Miller also had a favorite ploy for students who slept in class; he'd bring them to the experiment apparatus in the front of the hall. "Now, just hold on to this bar," he'd say to the victim -- then send an electric current through the bar. By the time the sleeper recovered, he was too concerned about any other such devices in the lecture hall to allow himself to doze once more.

Such tactics today would be considered affronts to human rights, I suppose -- yet they helped establish one prof's personality in class... and I recall him with a rather curious fondness, certainly not malevolence.

But, then, I was never called up to the front during a lecture.

I found "up front" in other ways, sometimes with equal fascination. For instance, during my 36 years at Mount Union, I have also served on our local city school board. Somebody suggested that I "get involved," and, by golly, I was elected. It seemed appropriate that I conduct myself in a thoroughly professional manner, offering only what an academically-minded person could: wise judgment, wise counsel, and very wise behavior at all meetings.

Surrounded by extremely competent persons (one of them a former student of mine) I was elected to the presidency of the school board, the epitome of progressive leadership. I whirled about in public meetings, banged the gavel with dexterity, was a go-between for citizen complaints -- and thought of myself as a shining example for the teachers. We had just gotten approval for a new high school building and were seeking additional favors from the Ohio State Board of Education for funding to ensure a complete vocational wing. Dick Hamrick, our superintendent, had assured the local board that the January meeting of the State Board was the crucial one for us to attend, to lobby for our cause.

Early in December of 1971 I was giving a final examination in freshman English when a secretary came in, told of an "emergency" call for me. The class was hopeful it was a dire circumstance; perhaps my wife had left me or the furnace had exploded. It was neither. The superintendent was calling; the State Board was in special session that very morning on vocational funding and we had to get to Columbus immediately to testify.

"I'm giving a final examination!"

"What do you want -- a full gradebook or a new vocational wing at the high school?"

A chartered Piper twin-engined Cherokee whisked us to the capitol where our strategy was to rebut whatever others were saying. Entering, we were asked if we "wished to give testimony." Paper was thrust at me to sign. I had no better surface on which to write, so I cradled the paper in my hand and scribbled "Lyle Crist" quickly, then "Alliance Board President" and "Testimony on vocational funding." We entered a huge room with Michelangelo on the walls and 400 persons gathered, listening to the august State Board of Education which controlled $72,000,000 that day. No empty seats. We huddled in a dark corner, Dick saying, "Listen carefully and then we'll rebut."

I still had my topcoat on, ear cocked to the podium, when the testifier said, "That, gentlemen, concludes my testimony." Apparently we would have missed the entire meeting if we'd arrived five minutes later -- because the President, holding a piece of paper in his hand, said, "The next to speak... will be ... will be..." His pause was momentous. "I can't make out his name, but he is the president of the Alliance city board."

"Go get 'em Tiger." The superintendent was extremely helpful.

How could I rebut a "That concludes my testimony"? Someone took my coat and shoved me toward the platform.

This is a tale about divinity and humility. They go together. I was supposed to say something which would put our school in the right light. A dignified, helpful position. How to make such a lofty impression? Pacing myself, I proceeded to the front of the auditorium; all eyes on the English prof who couldn't write his name clearly enough for another to read a simple "Lyle Crist."

I heard the president try again. "Could it ... could it..." He was alternately looking at the paper and then at me.

With all eyes in focus now, the crowd emotionally set, the President struggled again, finally asking, "Could it be *Christ*?"

Would anyone offer a rebuttal to that?

The fact that our school system was granted $2.1 million that day for a vocational wing concludes the story. The defense rests. And is quite humble in retrospect.

Humbling thus occurs in classroom, on road jaunts in civic interests -- and on the telephone, too. It happens when some faculty members undertake to assist the admissions office. There were hard times for small, privately supported schools in the 1960s; Kent State was not content with its 25,000-student main campus a shot-put away. It built for 5,000 students a branch 15 miles east of Mount, another branch 20 miles west for 10,000 students, and another 38 miles south for 6,000 students. At one time, back in the days when little Mount Union played the University of Michigan in football (losing horribly, but it must have been exciting), the college was the only one of its kind in the area. But by 1970 we were surrounded by friendly enemies. And we began to recruit with a bit of desperation, trying out new techniques. The faculty, for example, was asked to assist by taking bundles of green computer cards with names of prospective students, names culled from high school bulletin boards, from inquiries made by third cousins, and names garnered during street corner conversations.

I have never had much luck with them. We were to call these far-away numbers, introduce ourselves as important faculty members, show the prospective students that we really care -- impress them with the fact that genuine, red-blooded professors are making the calls.

"Hello there; is this the residence of Junior Raymond Philabaum of 2243 South Plum Street in Oskatoo, Montana?"

"What's it to you?"

I am in my study at home. Outside it is raining.

"Hi there! This is Professor Crist from Mount Union College. I am a member of the English department and I just wanted to let Junior know that I am really interested in having him in my classes some day next year."

"Whatya selling?"

"Nothing. Nothing at all. I teach full time at the College and I understand that Junior Raymond Philabaum has expressed an interest in our fine campus. I am calling from Ohio where the College is located to see if I can be of any assistance."

"You selling TV Guide subscriptions, ain't you?"

I think about becoming a bank teller. Anything other than teaching in college. I once knew a bank president and maybe someone in his family would remember me if interviewed. "Not really, sir. I am a professor--"

"You want to talk to Junior?"

"Well, yes, I'd be delighted to talk with him. I understand he is a fine young man truly interested in higher education."

"He's out boozing right now with some floozie. You got snow on your campus?"

"Not much." But the clouds are becoming more oppressive. "How are things in Montana?"

"Snow. What else? You got any special prices on *Sports Illustrated?*"

"Not really, sir. I am a full professor of English. Perhaps I can call back and talk to Junior another time. We take a deep personal interest in our students at Mount Union College and I'd be happy to discuss the English program--"

"Yeah. You just do that."

The phone jars. He has hung up. I have thirteen more green computer cards to check out this evening. A smile, however, begins to appear. I toss the collection in the wastebasket and tomorrow I'll say that my phone has been out of order. Tomorrow I will also make application for a teaching job at Kent State. Any branch will do.

The humbling has come in diverse ways. Textbook research is fine in its place, but if the prof gets a chance to travel he surely finds out about regionalisms in a more impressive -- and humbling -- way than from page 416 of a stuffy tome. It happened to me at Caldwell College in North Carolina in 1975.

Speaking to a group of area writers and teachers, I gave a stirring account of symbolism in American literature. My model was Glenway Wescott's short novel *The Pilgrim Hawk*, a tale of a failing marriage. The wife has taken up the sport of falconry and carries a hawk tethered to her arm. When she wishes, she releases the bird which then makes its swoop on some assigned object, returns with the booty, and assumes its place again on her well-positioned arm; the chain goes back on the bird's leg.

"This is, of course, a very obvious symbol for the plight of the woman's husband," I pointed out. "The woman is the dominant character, the man a weakling, trained in a way just as the bird is -- to be chained, then to respond on command."

I was in good form that night. But I dwelled on a certain phrase too long.

"You can picture this woman carrying around a hawk on her arm. Just picture that: she has a hawk on her arm, a hawk chained to her arm. Unusual, yes -- but so very effective for the symbolic purpose intended."

I was about to learn a lesson in something more important than symbolism.

Several in the audience began to titter; I noticed that the Caldwell professor who had invited me to give this lecture was among those who moved a bit restlessly; she did not cover her broad grin.

"So the woman with the hawk, carrying around the hawk on her arm, becomes a meaningful device in the unfolding of the larger story." I finished the lecture and followed the others into the reception area. Cornering the department chairwoman, I asked about the time of rustling in the audience, the repressed titters and her own wide grin. "What was going on?"

I had suspected someone in the audience had been passing around sleazy photographs perhaps.

She laughed. "Oh, you really got everybody going on that bit about the woman and the bird!"

"Yes?" I was about to be humbled.

"Well, down here in the Carolinas the bird is pronounced "houk" -- a houk flies in the air. You see, Lyle, the only "hock" we have around here is a ham hock -- and the entire audience was giggling over your dramatic word picture of the woman going around with a hamhock chained to her arm. Frankly, the symbol made the wrong impression "

I nodded weakly, vowing to return to Caldwell College only at a much higher fee.

In the Leamington Hotel in Minneapolis back in 1968 I joined others for the National Council of Teachers of English convention. At such meetings the chief informal discussions are on how to improve one's status and the chief formal sessions are on scholarly papers designed to achieve that status.

I delivered a stirring paper, one touching on new skills in writing, motivation, analysis -- and a final dash of personal approach in the classroom. In the 30 minutes allotted to me before some 200 other professors who decided to listen in, I was witty, exciting, entertaining. The gentleman who had introduced me laughed heartily at the right times; afterwards he had to wait his turn as many others clamored around me. I was in my glory.

Finally he was able to reach me. Flashing a handful of evaluation sheets, he said, "Just great! You went over beautifully! Like to see these evaluations?"

He thrust them into my hands, confident of response. I was delighted; some 40 persons had taken the time to fill out the sheets and all were full of praise for my somewhat unorthodox paper and performance. Then I noticed the one paper still in the introducer's hand.

"What about that one?" I was eager for the capstone compliment.

"Well, it's just another." He started to leave.

"Let me take a look." I knew it had to be the best. And so I read it. Written diagonally across the page, ignoring the stated categories, was the large scrawl of some fellow professor:

"I think Crist is a fake."

The scene still haunts me. Decades have passed but I'm very much aware that out there somewhere is a professor who holds that judgment about this olde English prof. Well, maybe I am a put-on. Maybe all teaching is. Technology must be accurate even if it is not interesting, but teaching must be interesting -- even if we round out a few corners. It would be accurate merely to stand in front of a class and read aloud the wisdom from some textbook (written perhaps by an "old codger!") and let that be the entire story. But I doubt that classes would retain that extra dimension of insight and curiosity unless the profs did a bit more. Sometimes an element of the dramatic can bring rewards.

There were 15 students in the creative writing class a decade after the NCTE judgment; we met in a tight little seminar room, writing poetry. Or trying to. I was terribly upset on this particular day because all their poems were so uniformly dull and general. How can you do justice to a topic such as "life" in four lines? Their poems were vague abstractions -- "gaseous" is the term I used.

"I'm weary of this stuff," I announced. "You people write 'The world is large and I am small. Why was I born?' This is not poetry: it is gas. Obviously the world is large and obviously we are small in structure by comparison. Everybody knows that; you've neither said the obvious in a new way nor said anything new. This is not poetry. It is gunk."

I added, with a bit of a flourish, "And if you don't know why you were born come to my office this afternoon." Getting a head of steam now, I raved on: "I don't want to see any more of this drivel."

I am striding toward the seminar door. "In fact, I don't want to see anything of this class at all until somebody in here writes one decent poem about something simple and mundane." At the door now.

I clutched the doorknob. A metallic spheroid, cold, hard, merely useful.

I wanted to make a point.

Squeezing the thing, I kept a grim visage.

"Until somebody writes a poem about something as poetic as a doorknob."

With that I left, slamming the door, striding to the office, and realizing that I might never meet the class again. What if no one wrote about a specific, mundane doorknob? I visioned the college trustees trying to figure out in special session how to dismiss me without a legal hassle.

"Prof. Crist actually left the classroom--"

"And never returned. All winter long the students came to class. They waited and waited for six weeks!"

"Strange. He taught all his other classes. Just never paid any attention to this one."

"Obviously an unbalanced man."

"Probably a fake."

The trustees would take a secret ballot, ultimately recommend that I have professional help. AA, perhaps -- start on Academicians Anonymous. But something else happened. That evening the doorbell rang at my home; Tom Gorham, basketball player, class member who seldom opened his mouth other than to shout "dunk!" was at the door. I had him pegged as a C plus student -- though I did look up to him. He thrust a small piece of paper at me and made a speech.

"Here," he said. He left immediately, I looked at the paper. It was a poem, titled *Doorknob*.

> Hey doorknob,
> what can you tell me?
> I can tell you, boy,
> about sweat and grease
> and a mother gently peeking in
> on her sleeping baby girl,
> slams and twists
> and the time we had
> housebreaking the dog,
> tugs and pulls
> and the oldest son home from the Army:
> "Surprise, Mom! I love you!"

Beautiful! A simple doorknob full of specific implications. How could the dog ever get to the yard in time if there were no doorknob?

I met the class the next afternoon. I had come close to disastrous dramatics, but the message had gotten through to Tom. He did the work -- and we all learned from it.

The humbling experience for a prof may come from overconfidence, too. In 1980, for instance, I taught a special group of 21 Japanese coeds from Baika College in Osaka -- at Mount Union to enrich their awareness of American literature. Into the second week of discussion of Mark Twain, Mitsuku Yamamoto came into class wearing a Mickey Mouse T-shirt. I commented on the fact that Mickey was no longer the great American cartoon figure -- that Wile E. Coyote had earned the position now.

"Mickey Mouse is a bit passe."

"Passe?" Ah!

Faces contorted. The girls checked their dictionaries. This led to explanations both of "passe" and of "coyote." The coyote appeared in their dictionaries in a conventional drawing. I said, "The coyote in the famed roadrunner-coyote cartoons is an exaggerated figure; but he is genuine Americana, coming from our western states."

I collect coyote memorabilia; I am prejudiced. I had 21 coyote stick figures, drawings, puppets, stuffed toys, and plastic figures on my office shelves. Other faculty members place scholarly books on their shelves. I hurried to the office around the corner, grabbed a coyote puppet, then showed it to the Japanese girls. "Take a look. This is the genuine Americana. Mice are everywhere, but the coyote is special for America." I went on, not realizing the hole I was digging for myself.

Mitsuku, holding the puppet now, fondling it, suddenly cried, "Missa Crist! Missa Crist!" She gestured for me to come to her side.

"Yes?" Assuming that she had something scholarly to point out to me, I continued singing the American praises of the coyote cartoon figure. She pointed feverishly to the coyote puppet and said, "Looka here!"

I eyed the neck of the puppet. Imprinted in very large capital letters were these words: "MADE IN JAPAN." At that point I realized more forcibly than ever before the dilemma we face with Datsun, Toyota, and Honda. Teaching, as I have noted, is a humbling experience.

You have a brand new brief case by Hartmann Luggage. Five inches deep, ideal for many papers, nice and wide, yet it can be stored under the airline seat. Handy, efficient. Why, there are two thin flaps which you grasp at either side, press onto a receiving buttons to firmly lock the exterior design, covering the open-shut mechanism. The flaps dress up the case, adding the final decorator touch. However, you forget to button one flap because the case is new and you're in a hurry as you leave the third-floor office in Chapman Hall. The flap dangles.

You rush to the elevator, nod at the young coed who is in the elevator. She's not in any of your classes, but you exchange pleasant glances briefly, then stare at your shoes as the elevator slowly descends. You hold your new briefcase -- the one that clicks nicely and has additional small flaps which snap at the corners. And five seconds later your life is shattered as the coed very deliberately speaks.

"Your thing is open."

No other single segment of your academic career is as disordered as the next ten seconds, as you ponder whether to thank the young lady, reach down and shamelessly check your zipper, or turn slowly and face the wall. The coed leaves on the first floor. You do not get out. The door closes and your proceed with the sanitary genuflect -- and then see the dangling flap on the new Hartmann brief case.

Teaching is a humbling experience.

Remember those "pop" quizzes? Those unannounced brief tests that the prof would spring from time to time -- to see if the class had been doing the required reading?

In 1985 I became a grandfather for the first time. I wanted to celebrate after I got the phone call that October evening. .. and so I decided to give a "gram-pop" quiz in American literature class the next morning.

They weren't ready for it. After all, we had had a full-hour test just a few days before...and no prof ever gives a quiz so soon after a scheduled test!

But I distributed the gram-pop quiz -- and received many blank pages from the class. Few had read the assignment. But one young lady should make a fine attorney some day. At the bottom of an otherwise blank page, she wrote these memorable words:

> "Prof. Crist -- do you realize that if I flunk this
> class I will have to enroll in another one of your classes
> in the spring semester. Is that really what you want?"

Michelle Cline signed her name. I decided not to count the grades that day.

It is a humbling experience, this teaching business! But some times the prof learns more than he at first realizes. Go back 25 years. The sophomore sat across from me in the office, impressing me more for her candid honesty than scholarly potential. "Sometimes in class I feel like a fool. I just don't seem to follow your explanations about prose and poetry mixing."

I nodded. "I want you to see that poetry is not all iambic pentameter. It's there in good fiction. How are your other studies?"

"Better. I understand history."

Routine inquiry. "You're a sophomore?"

She nodded. "McMaster Hall?"

"Third floor, north. Second on the right."

I offered some small talk. "I like the start of classes in the fall. I was coming across campus last night, past the library, then the dorms. There's something good about lights on, even though just in some of the rooms."

"I hate lights in the rooms." She spoke with suddenness. "They give me the creeps."

"Oh?"

"Lights in a girls' dorm on Friday. Some girl is probably alone, without a date. Chances are she's the one who needs a date most of all."

This was at a time when only the women were allowed in the women's dorm rooms, when there were social standards on campus now thought of as archaic. Her eyes moved to the papers on my desk. Her own, on top, with a bold "D" in the margin. Almost in apology, I said, "grades don't mean everything."

"I tried to answer the question. I just don't follow the reasoning, I guess."

"The point simply is that poetry does come in fiction. Human sensitivities, rich expression."

She was trying. "I didn't answer that, did I?"

"You referred to rhymes and meters. But it's also poetic when Tom Joad drives that battered truck to the migrant camp, past fellow workers being beaten. They plead his aid, and on the other side of the road is a man flagging him to turn into camp if he's to get any work. Pathos in *The Grapes of Wrath* is capsuled in his desperate, single word: 'Where?' Where is he to go? To get work or to aid his friends? He cannot have both."

She smiled. "I suppose there was no specific meter in his phrasing."

Then, so easily, I went on. "I once wrote a story in which I symbolized the message with a house with open windows. Like eyes." I paused, then became the wise old prof again. "There was a girl in the house, longing to break away. She got her chance when a knight in armor, so to speak, came by -- but she had to leave against the will of her ruthless father. Unknown to the knight, she kills her father, rushes upstairs to grab belongings. On a window sill is an open can of paint, red paint. Someone had been painting the trim. Do you see my symbol developing?" That was important.

"The knight -- he didn't know about the murder?"

"No."

"She's tried to get away before?"

"I'd sense that. The house holds her. The tyrannical father is responsible." I went on. "What would you have happen now to symbolize her futility?"

"Well, the girl probably spills the paint accidentally -- out the window."

"And?"

"And the knight sees it."

"What does it look like?"

"Like blood. Running down the side of the house."

Hurrying now. "Out of the eye. It's the murder symbolized." "What else does it say to the knight?"

"The house is wounded. It's either the end of the house or the girl's way of life, or --" I did not interrupt. "Or it drives him away. Symbolizes evil. The very thing she did to get him will now lose him."

"It's mechanical, of course. Overdone -- or I would have had it published in *Harper's* instead of a very minor quarterly!" Then, as a benediction, I added, "John Ciardi said we should never paraphrase a poem to try to explain it -- when we do we lose the poem. You have to experience the story as you read it."

The work of literary masters; that's what I'm paid to teach and I had used a story of my own. I am a lousy prof.

She left. Feeling a bit guilty, pondering, I went back to work, tried to drum up interest in a paper for a College English Association meeting. Then home, supper, then back to the desk. It was past nine o'clock that Friday evening when I decided to call it quits. I walked across campus. Nearing the north side, I found myself pondering scattered lights, a brief galaxy in campus world. And then I noticed the third floor, in the center of McMaster Hall -- a solitary light there, second on the right, brighter than the sprinkling of others dotting walls.

I pictured her trying to read a book, making small talk, precious sophomore hours slipping away. *They give me the creeps*, she had said. I had told her of a gossamer experience of awareness -- and now a symbol was returning to me. One light far better than a can of red paint spilled across a house.

It was, indeed, the experiencing of it.

The symbols are all around us.

I keep learning from the young women and young men who make poetry every day, all the time ... going right to the heart of the world just by being themselves.

It *is* a humbling experience, this profession of teaching.

Humbling in a very precious way.

4

Take the Stars With You

Literature Prof

The text had 187 short stories
and two cartons of poems
(and there were more than 100 pieces
of asphalt tile on the floor in the room;
I started counting them one day)
as I said, there were 287 short stories
and three cartons of poems and
I tried to show what makes a story click
a poem mean something
and I said, "See the cyclic effect
in this story by Trilling? a cycle of events
and we begin where we end
and we see the use of setting in 'Open Boat'
by Crane because the sea is unsafe
and land is security
and all four men must move from danger to safety.
And that is good use of setting.
And look at the richness of simple reference
in Axe Helves. "Imagine! A man
spending his life molding axe helves!
But he knows there is a right one for each man
and that is rich use of simple reference."
Pry open minds, wedge wisdom

so that they can see *for themselves* how it is
with literature.

Well, with 387 short stories
and four cartons of poems in our text
it was examination time and I asked
all that I could ask:
"From 487 short stories and five cartons of poems
discuss use of cycle in stories,
tell me about useful setting, describe some
simple poetic reference that is rich
in universal meaning."
And paper and paper and paper and paper
came in for grading and they say,
"See! How well we know our lesson." They write
"See the cyclic effect in the story by Trilling,
the story ends where it had begun and what
better setting could there by than land
and sea as in 'Open Boat' for here
the sea is danger and land is safety;
how useful, how appropriate it is."
They say, "And there is no better poetry of
simple reference than 'Axe Helve' by Frost
for here is a man dedicated to molding an
axe-helve to the man, spending his life
for such a proposition!"
And the papers summarize, "Truly this course
has given me wisdom and understanding and
awareness, for now I can discern what
literature is and I am much better for having
been in your class."
I am desolate;
but with 587 short stories and six cartons
of poems in the text
I will meet another class next term.

Ah! I am afraid that soon I shall
do no more
than count the tiles
on the floor.

That's the trouble with some teaching techniques; they come back to haunt you by depriving the student of the vitality of learning for himself. We get so involved in names, dates, tricks of the trade -- and all are necessary, of course -- we lose sight of the next and important steps in reading clearly -- that of individual perception. There is no valid reason why students must always mimic the prof, feed back just what has been pointed out. We can teach map-reading and surely no student who has used a map of New York state in class will take one of California later on, glibly pointing out Long Island, Rochester, and the Adirondack Mountains.

But it happens in literature. And when feedback rehearsed in class is all that counts, we have lost the grand experience of personal discernment. At some point -- beyond gradebooks and class discussions -- that self-discernment is tremendously important.

Kahlil Gibran's words are regularly used in my classes: "The teacher who is wise does not lead you to his chambers of wisdom, but rather to the threshold of your own..." No educational theory which simply appropriates one person's experience for another's makes sense.

A teacher does not give wisdom: he gives time, love, patience, sweat -- but never his mentality, for what good is something which the student cannot claim for his own?

There's another aspect. Ken Chalker, a 1971 graduate, now a minister in Cleveland, reminded me. After reading *Literature Prof* he wrote me, "Is it not possible that for a while a student has no choice but to respond as a parrot? Maturing and building a personal intellectual frame of reference from which to interpret and respond to life's events and routines has hardly begun during the college years."

Ken concluded, "Professors may in fact hear the sound of the parrot, but the parrot, in some cases, is beginning to learn how to think."

Sidney Cox, in a little book on writing titled *Indirections*, said something about learning via imitation: "Soon ideas of your own will appear, as chickadees and juncoes do when seeds are scattered on the snow." All too often the tiles on the floor seem to dominate. If, however, the threshold of the young mind is gained through imitation, then perhaps the tiles serve their purpose well. "A personal intellectual frame of reference" -- Ken's phrasing; terribly important. So much so that we are closing in on the rock bottom question of motivation.

Pete Stewart came to the office in 1976 after a session on Ralph Waldo Emerson. The essay on *Nature* is not an easy one to read, leading as it does to what Emerson calls a "noble doubt" that matter exists other than as an extension of thought. The class session had been dull, I imagine. I rambled on, pointed out passages, asked questions -- and got few answers. We struggled mightily but brought down nothing more than the 60 minutes allotted for the class.

"Of course, you rely on grades for motivation," Pete said. "I understand that. We read and go to class to see what questions you'll ask and then we make note of the answers which you give us when we don't answer."

Wise young man. Too bad he is a music major.

"I don't think that's the best motivation. There's grade motivation and then there's teacher motivation --"

"Explain."

"Well, the kind that comes from your own example. You do set an example -- and a prof's enthusiasm for the subject spurs some in the class to read more deeply. To catch on."

This from a music major, mind you.

"But the best kind is self-motivation. The motivation that gets us to read because we want to read."

The conversation which followed was strong on agreement, weak on further insights regarding the chemistry of getting that self-motivation generated. There's no doubt that those without motivation are the sorriest lot. Apathy is the heaviest burden anyone can bear. Timothy Healy, president of Georgetown University, told prep schoolers some years ago that "if the college you go to is any good, it will hit you like a ton of bricks. It will lead you to question every conclusion you have ever reached; it will lead you to deny lots of assumptions and remake them; it will refuse to answer many of your questions because you're asking the wrong ones." He added, "You will be stretched till you squawk."

That evening, after the talk with Pete, I was rummaging around in my thought, banging into preconceptions, fiddling with long-held judgments, when I recalled a manuscript Dave Nartonis was working on, something titled *Self Education*. Dave taught a course at Principia College in Illinois where I serve occasionally on a summer school staff; his course on perception always drew much interest. Digging around in the manuscript, shoveling away, I found part of the problem of the ho-hum situation. I'd known it all along, but hadn't been able to really put my finger on it.

According to Nartonis, the problem is that students generally do not know how to ask questions. It isn't a "natural" involvement for them; the questioning process becomes even hazier in the reading and studying of relatively heavy materials, deeper ideas. Yet asking is absolutely essential if we're to have any sense of self-education -- and self-motivation.

Basically, Nartonis asks for analysis, synthesis, and hypothesis to be the bases, the roots, of all questions. Analysis involves questions of the details, the parts, the qualities. When we synthesize, we ask what are the relationships, the contexts, the functions. And when we hypothesize we ask about the possibilities -- and the different ways in which facts may be interpreted. We learn by stretching our experience.

Nartonis tells of a fish who, when asked what water was, did not know. However, several days later when the fish was found dangling on the line, the fish knew considerably more about water than ever before. It was, in fact, something of an extension of itself -- a necessary component.

And so we come back to Emerson who wrote, "Nature is made to conspire with spirit to emancipate us. Certain mechanical changes, a small alteration in our local position apprises us of dualism."

We relate and synthesize our experiences -- and the prof should be of assistance. The young woman in the late 1960s at Mount whose T-shirt read "I want to make my own mistakes" missed the point.

A prof is supposed to help minimize the mistakes by a little guiding -- and leading. Nature conspires. It teaches lessons of patience and learning. And a prof should follow that example, by being such an example. We appreciate beauty which is nature; we pick the flowers, arrange them, imitate nature's patterns in architecture; we emulate nature and by that process we compliment and reinforce it. Let the prof compliment the students -- and the students will listen more carefully. We all need a word of appreciation, even old professors, when they're teaching the writings of Emerson!

In 1987, for instance, I assigned my literature class to read his classic essay on Self Reliance. It's full of witticisms, of unique images, and certainly of down-to-earth suggestions which I figured all young persons would appreciate. Lines such as, "Trust thyself; every heart beats to that iron string"... and "What I must do is all that concerns me, not what society says..."

In between, alas, are some rather long sentences, some philosophical musings, and historical references which have not the vibrancy of punk rock. Recitation was a disaster. Nobody had finished the essay, nobody understood it, nobody really cared.

"It's all so boring," one young woman said. "Why do we have such dull stuff?"

I had no answer, other than to point out that I had thought it would be at least of interest to them. The 39 members of the class filed out of the room in utter apathy.

The mother of one of my colleagues in the biology department had been auditing the class. She came up to the desk and said what undoubtedly needed to be said to me.

"I found the essay lots of fun. I really appreciated it. Excellent points."

Then Mrs. Epp paused. "But, well, when I was their age, I, too, would have found it boring." She smiled hesitantly, then walked to the door.

The artistry, the literature. It's hard to define. And I need to learn that it needs interaction with others. A wider perspective.

Artistry is in this poem of another 19th century writer. Walt Whitman found beauty in a Louisiana oak tree, growing alone, solitary in an open field, putting forth beautiful green leaves -- "uttering" them, as he wrote:

> I saw in Louisiana a live-oak growing,
> All alone stood it and the moss hung down from the branches,
> Without any companion it grew there uttering joyous leaves of dark green
> And its look, rude, unbending, lusty, made me think of myself,
> But I wondered how it could utter joyous leaves standing alone there without its friends near, for I know I could not.
> And I broke off a twig with a certain number of leaves upon it, and twined around it a little moss,
> And brought it away, and have placed it in sight, in my room.
> It is not needed to remind me of my own dear friends,
> (For I believe lately I think of little else but them)
> Yet it remains for me a curious token, it makes me think of manly love;

>For all that, and though the live-oak glistens there in Louisiana, solitary in a wide flat space,
>Uttering joyous leaves all its life without a friend or lover near,
>I know very well I could not.

The poem is a dualistic expression, placing the tree next to Whitman's own conclusions. Whitman observed. Then he interpreted. Then he concluded.

Profs at all grades earn their salary when they can be their own example, provide the motivation for students to observe and inquire, interpret and speculate. The deadliest classroom is the one which offers no questions.

B.F. Maiz was a man in his mid sixties, most of the years spent behind bars for a variety of offenses. Later, he wrote poems, reading them on campuses. Seventeen years ago I heard him say to our students, "You want an education? Man, I never had no education. I got hassled with the wrong stuff -- but I learned something. It took me fifty years to realize this, but I learned something about getting an education, and I'm going to tell you about it now. You are here on this fine campus and I never went past the fifth grade, yet here I am telling you how to get an education -- and it won't cost you a penny."

I sat in Presser Recital Hall wondering what this man could say that would be of meaning, a man who had no formal academic training at all.

"You want an education? You *ask questions*! That's all! Ask 'em everywhere. Ask 'em of everybody. And you listen to all the answers. And then you put 'em together and think for yourself."

Probably as significant a statement as any speaker ever made on the Mount Union campus!

B.F. Maiz added, "You know why I spent half my life behind bars? I never asked questions!"

He had grown up in a ghetto, was on the streets at early age, never questioned anything the other fellows said they'd do that day. Went along with the crowd, never questioning -- until one day, in his fifties, in jail, he began to realize what he had missed.

The T-shirt had said "I want to make my own mistakes." But how many?

"Computers can answer virtually anything," Maiz said. "But it can't ask questions."

Students can. Motivated, they can. But too often silence reigns. The prof, after assigning fifty pages to be read, enters, eyeballs the class, and opens the discussion for questions stemming from those fifty pages. Silence takes over. An awkward one, eyes are on shoes, shuffles disturb the calm, but there are no questions. To ask would be to suggest "points" -- trying to favor the prof, toady -- or to prolong the class period. Or to show ignorance. None is acceptable.

Richard Armour tells of teaching in Germany during the early part of Nazi regime -- how the professors would gather for a full fifteen minutes of the class session before entering their respective classrooms. Late entrance showed superiority; students had to wait. And the "Heil Hitler" salute would follow. And questions were taboo. Asking questions might get at truths. Why, even the superiority of the professors might be questioned!

Yet truth is no on-the-shelf commodity; it is appreciated only when examined, bounced, juggled, shared, Sometimes it is the prof who must start the questioning. I've found that rather than some testy poser about an author's judgment on page 556 of the text, it's better to remember that *intrigue* is the common denominator we have -- even if we're not all authorities (or wish to be) on some nineteenth century poet. We are authorities on love, fear, anger, decision-making; let these come first. Why would you write about God and never use the term "God"? Do you recall any bittersweet time in your early years? The first can lead to "Thanatopsis" by Bryant, the second to "My Papa's Waltz" by Theodore Roethke -- and their poems become more meaningful than memory work.

The opportunity in teaching is the combining of the prof's superior mental experience with the equal mental potential of students. Sometimes we need to continue uttering those joyous leaves without others being aware of them.

This would not appeal to everyone. It takes a special breed to be a teacher. Degrees, essential, are not the chief ingredient. Attitude is about as important as knowledge. I'm saddened by the phrasing -- and attitude -- of a teacher who, while making legitimate complaint about back pay in her career in a large city system beset with financial problems, spoke of her training in a letter to the editor this way:

"I and countless others have already made a four-year financial, emotional and mental sacrifice to prepare ourselves for the field of education..."

Sacrifice?

Those four years of higher education should have been rewarding, invigorating -- a stimulating sequence, perhaps the best in a lifetime. Finances were taxed, of course, but the phrase "mental sacrifice" is a cop-out. I am happy that my children did not have to be in a classroom of this unfortunate "teacher" who looks upon the vital, active preparation for her career as a mental sacrifice. What, I would ask, was ever lost?

We never deal with things; it is always people. We need to be reminded of the uniqueness of the academy. In the early 1970s a letter came to me from a high school junior in southern Ohio. She had been responsive to some points I made during an assembly program in her high school and we had corresponded. Her English teacher had made an assignment which she accepted fully:

"Write about some specific person you know. Be honest and candid as you express your thoughts about that person's character, habits, personality -- what makes you unhappy as well as what pleases you."

The school was small, in a rural area. Taking this into account, the teacher added, "Don't worry about anything you say which might be negative in any way. I assure you no one will see your theme except me. Strictly confidential."

So Heidi followed instructions, poured out a paper descriptive of her mother; she told of some of her mother's rough edges as well as her beauty. She did not ignore the faults; there were candid, open judgments. Heidi felt she appreciated vocabulary more than ever as she worked out the best ways to make points she had in mind.

It wasn't the grade which bothered her. It was the teacher's betrayal; he took the paper to Heidi's mother. Anguish, misunderstandings, confusion followed. Heidi wrote to this far-off English prof, "What will I do? My mom is terribly upset with me because I just tried to be honest, like my teacher said. Now she thinks I don't love her."

Perhaps she wrote me feeling I was far enough away that I could do no further harm. In reply I said, "Your teacher is not a teacher. He is unfit for the classroom -- and we must pity him." I gave some thoughts to encourage Heidi to continue dialogue with her mother, adding that "Your problem, however great, is not as severe as the one your teacher has. Let you and your mother find common ground in awareness of the inadequacy of that person who needs help far more than you do."

I hope today that he is a teacher. If he is a teacher, he is honest. If he is not honest, he should he removed from his post. Of course, I'm interpreting as I think back over this incident. I've taken the basic circumstances, analyzed them, now I have synthesized them to form my opinion. He may have thought he was doing the family a favor -- that could have been his synthesis. If so, he needed to speculate a bit further on the consequences. We all need to do that.

Teachers are the objects of much venting of emotion. They ought to be in such a case as Heidi's. But we can laugh at some of the other ways. I don't know the details at Yale in the late 19th century, but I do know that William Randolph Hearst, to become our great newspaper tycoon, was expelled from Yale for his own venting. He was creative, too. In an era without mass plumbing facilities in the dorms, chamber pots were in each room, discreetly stored under the beds. Hearst, for some unknown but apparently good reason, painted portraits of a number of key professors -- inside the chamber pots.

He was saying something about each one. Yale expelled him, however, when his message was discovered -- and fully comprehended!

Come back to Emerson. That gentleman left more meaningful messages for professors, all teachers. One, perhaps as significant as any, came out of a cave in northwestern Kentucky.

Along with six other companions, Emerson in the mid-nineteenth century had occasion to explore some of the Mammoth Cave. With flares they moved inside, poked around, went more and more deeply into the cavern. Then six extinguished their flares, leaving the faint glow of but one to illuminate the large area where they were. Emerson looked up -- and saw stars.

Now, how could he actually see stars in the heavens when he was 75 or 100 feet below ground, inside the cave? Yet he wrote that there were beautiful stars in the night-time sky. In reality, they were stones, a few with high reflective quality, shimmering in the dim glow of the single flare. But to Emerson's eye they were more! They were the stars in a beautiful ebon sky.

Unlike many persons, Emerson was intrigued by this phenomenon -- and thought about it. When he got to the point of putting words on paper, he said, "Our first mistake is to think that the circumstance brings the joy, which we always bring to the circumstance."

He had brought the "joy" with him -- as remembrance of stars in the night sky; as he did, the "circumstance" of being in a cave below the earth's surface, with shimmering stones, all this took on the added beauty of the stars and sky. But they were not stars; it was

Emerson's mind, his thought, his own activity which he took with him and applied to the cavern.

There is a lesson in this for teachers, for all of us. Having a good day on campus? Students behaving in high school? Tests getting better? Harmony with administration and parents? Obviously there is something to be said for the others involved -- but the role of the teacher bringing his own harmony, his own competency, his own skills into the cavern, the classroom, is most significant. Whenever this English prof took with him the awareness (beyond all the jokes and even the sarcasm) that his students are of intelligence, then I had meaningful sessions. My own attitude is the key one; I have to take the stars with me.

I do not always do that. But I know -- oh, how well I know! -- that I should! I enjoy poking fun at their antics, their ineptness in writing on occasion, but no prof should hold the thought of inferiority regarding students. If I see them as limited, I surely will limit in turn whatever teaching ability I have.

There was little beauty in Heidi's teacher's classroom because he failed to take the honesty of thought with him. The "joy" will come for him as he brings it with him, as he brings the beauty of integrity right into the cavern.

And that joy is seen again and again by teachers who know the deep significance of their work. Consider, for instance, one teacher in a large high school in south side Chicago many years ago. Geraldine Lawhorn was something of a mystery to all the teachers and students there -- for Gerry had, during her high school years, become both deaf and blind. What could she ever accomplish by staying in school?

One teacher made a world of difference. For Geraldine Lawhorn had loved poetry, loved literature, and although she could neither see nor hear, she could still share thoughts and poems she had memorized. One teacher at that school encouraged Gerry to put on a "performance" in her classroom.

"You come and recite some poems and tell them about what you've written," she encouraged the young girl.

Gerry told me, " I was so scared -- I really wanted to do this and I planned a full half-hour of it with enthusiasm, but I stood outside that classroom, shaking, so unsure of myself!"

The teacher led Gerry to the front of the room and introduced her. Gerry started. She could not hear herself speak. "I was trembling so," she told me. "I went through the whole presentation in about ten minutes!"

But that one teacher knew more could be accomplished. By touch she asked Gerry questions, told her to recite more poems -- and the deaf-blind girl began at last to find pleasure in the program.

"I loved it!" And then she said, "I made up my mind then that my goal in life would be to give a performance at Carnegie Hall!"

In the mid-1980s she became the 13th person in the world to earn a college degree while deaf and blind -- and she was in her 60s then. Today she teaches others who are handicapped, encouraging them, as her teacher had done, to achieve their highest goals.

Carnegie Hall? She got there. In fact, she performed twice at Carnegie Hall before moving on to the Hadley Correspondence School for the Blind.

One teacher had made the difference.

In our changeable society, with one family in five on the move, cross-nation flights in three hours, a language acceleration -- today our potential of words is twice that which Shakespeare had -- and with the pressures and frustrations of overpopulation and lack, there is ample need to encourage questions, express answers, and find the "beauty" of good activity in the classroom.

I wonder what my teacher friend at the NCTE convention would say about this prof stressing the beauty of teaching. Perhaps it is fakery for some. But, then, not all should be teachers. I think so often of Mark Twain's account of the difference between the beauty of the Mississippi River -- and the awareness of its forms purely in terms of usefulness.

He reveled in the beauty of the river prior to becoming a skilled navigator. The "broad expanse of the river" was blood red, the middle distance was "brightened into gold," a solitary log was "black and conspicuous," a long, slanting mark was "sparking in the water," and in another the surface was broken by "boiling, tumbling rings that were as many tinted as an opal," and high above a "clean-stemmed dead tree waves a single leafy bough that glowed like a flame in the unobstructed splendor that was flowing from the sun..."

After Twain learned to pilot a riverboat, however, the sun merely meant whether there would be rain tomorrow, the log merely meant the river was rising, the slanting mark merely meant a bluff reef was near, the tumbling boils merely showed a changing channel -- and the tall dead tree merely marked the miles traversed that day.

"The romance and the beauty were all gone from the river," Twain wrote. "All the value any feature of it had for me now was the amount of usefulness it could furnish..."

Students who become mere implements of a pay check are in rooms without beauty, they are merely means of a day's labor towards the grocery bill. Twain had to be a riverboat pilot for a living -- and so, too, teachers must survive. But can't we recognize the special dimension of beauty? That clumsy freshman is not merely a number on some printout sheet. Each student in his or her own special way brings beauty.

And even if the student is not aware of that right now, the prof should be a factor in bringing it to the surface. It can be done. Back in 1979 the Crist family rafted some 230 miles of the Colorado River through the Grand Canyon -- and saw not one bit of litter -- on the river, in camp grounds, along the shorelines or canyon walls. Expeditioners made it clear that we would take out every item we took with us on the week-long trek. Everybody on the trip got caught up in the excitement of keeping the natural beauty of that waterway. Every pop can top, every cigarette butt, every bit of tissue was always placed in trash bags, put back on the raft, removed from the scene.

People could keep all highways as well as their own streets just as clean if they recognized the beauty -- and the value of the beauty around them.

Profs and students can be just as well motivated, just as conscientious, keeping the classroom a place of intellectual beauty. They can, if they understand the rewards. I'm aware that Wordsworth once said, "I care little for the praise of any other professional but as it may help me to pudding." Well, we need the pudding. But teachers need beauty, too. If the beauty, the joy, does not seem to be there, we can always check our own remembered thought.

What are we bringing into the cavern -- the sense of the beauty of achievement or merely another day of the pudding?

Teachers have a special opportunity to manifest joy, so that others may better understand. Especially the students.

On to more of them now.

5

The Olde Prof

I'm asked, "Have college students changed much in recent years?"

Yes, they have. They're a lot younger. At least, the differential between their age and mine is much greater!

Students, further, are more sassy than they used to be. Today Jerry doesn't show up for class; I mark him absent. He pops in the next session. "You missed my class yesterday," I note.

"No, not at all."

He wouldn't have said that twenty years ago.

Moons ago when Mount Union was on the three-term system, I watched students coming back after Christmas break. My first contact was with Bruce, a towering, curly-headed sophomore who came to my office clutching his schedule card. "I see you're signed up for my journalism class." We'd be getting acquainted.

"Yeah, like, well, that's what I wanted to check on. Like, well, I got a question."

He received encouragement to proceed.

"Yeah, like, well, I got two hard subjects this term and, see, I need to know cause I can't really take three of them, you know what I mean? Like, if I stay in your class, well -- will I have to study?"

I ponder the manila folders on the desk, ones jammed with notes; I think of ideas captured over the break period, the Farber case, the journalistic struggle for access, freedom of information cases, the new texts, problems with the campus newspaper last term -- and the clippings which clutter my study at home.

"Yeah --" I find myself using his phrasing -- "like, you may have to study some. A teenie weenie. Nothing that will disturb you, though -- just regular writing assignments, layout, copyreadings, legal considerations and investigating."

"Man, I don't think I can handle all that."

Perhaps there is brightness somewhere. "The course is offered spring term as well. If you're hesitant why not take it then?"

"Like, naw I can't do that."

"Oh? Planning on skiing in the Alps then?"

"Naw, but, like, you got that class scheduled for first period in the spring. Like, that's 7:50 in the a.m.!"

Fingering tie folds nervously, I had to admit the truth in what he said. Outside the snow is building little ridges on the window pane.

"Like, no way can I handle Period I!"

Like I knew he was in Cunningham Hall, at least a block away from the classes. Like, baby, I understand.

We parted friends. May he find a job on the lobster shift should he ever make it to the daily press.

Well, what about coming to class? Should it be mandatory?

One Mount Union student put it this way on a questionnaire: "If the student doesn't want to attend class, that's his problem. This is not high school. If someone wants to waste his money by not taking advantage of his education and going to class, that's his fault, not mine or the prof's. Profs should not reduce a grade for non-attendance -- if the student blows off class he will suffer. We are adults and make our own decisions..."

A bit more eloquently, another wrote, "A student pays his king's ransom to attend Mount; why shouldn't he be allowed to decide on class attendance?"

Each prof at Mount sets his own grading standards, making them clear at the beginning of each term. My own approach, despite the usefulness of the expressions above, was to consider class attendance in the final grade. What happens in class is not merely a lecture on one hand nor a test on the other; it is a give and take of presentations, questions, responses; a dialogue. To be absent frequently is to miss participation in the dialogue -- and I don't know how to compensate for that. Why not get your money's worth? Ask questions, give input, be alive. So, my grades reflect attendance.

"There are 24 hours in every day. There are 168 hours in every week. When an individual pays $4,000 plus to go to school, 15 hours out of every week seems like a minuscule requirement..." That from another student of years ago. The figure became more than $12,000 in the 1980s.

Most attend. And poor is the prof who allows non-attendees to receive excellent grades. Students bring their own stars to the classroom cavern. They're needed; all the interpretations are important, every lecture period.

Values are evidenced in diverse ways.

Students brought the stars in 1967 when they realized that the snack bar at our new campus center was strong on pristine and loyal decor -- cinder block painted with the school colors of purple and white, with purple and white floor tile, and neat formica-top tables with aluminum chairs at each. We'd never had a snack bar before and this represented the very epitome of achievement. For some. For others, students who recognized crass commercialism, it was a place totally inappropriate for casual chatting, eating, and discussing. On the Student Life Committee that year the proposal came to have the students redecorate. What a grand group of students they were! Staying between terms, foregoing those between-term trips (some to Ft. Lauderdale because the beach movies were at their height then) to do something positive on campus.

Funded by the College, they put panels on those cinder block walls, built wooden booths to replace the tables, put down dull mottled green floor tile, painted the ceiling dark brown, put deep orange drapes over the windows, replacing the fancy, fringed ones, installed subdued lighting, placed deep-color plastic panels on the entrance doors (toning down the clear glass), and put a separation wall between the service counter and the booths. Everything made more sense with that.

And Mary Evelyn Weber, the president's wife, was there with them, helping sew the drapes, listening to the new ideas. There was a common sense of purpose. Wouldn't it be great if we had it at all other times!

The trauma we experienced in the spring of 1970 relates to attitudes and value judgments.

All evidence pointed to a conservative faction of fraternity students as having burned the two crosses on campus in the early morning hours of March 4 that year. Flag pole rallies, class takeovers, many confrontations took place. Serving then as chairman of the Student Life Committee -- a polyglot group of students, faculty and administration empowered to deal with social life on campus -- I found myself in the middle. The racial issue was, of course, dominant, but as I later learned there was an undercurrent not really racial in significance at all. The apparent issue was the Student Senate's rejection of a request by the Black Students Union for more funding. The cross burnings occurred after a heated meeting on that Monday evening in Chapman Hall, pointing fingers at those who had been most disturbed by the BSU request.

In retrospect, it is clear to me that these students had nothing to do with the cross burnings; the matches were struck by a small core of non-conservatives, in fact, who found through this a way to express their unhappiness with the college, Viet Nam, and the whole fabric of society that year.

False bomb scares were part of their tactics, and when the KSU tragedy took place we had already had visits by delegations from that campus, ready to assist the downtrodden on our campus, ready to "tear up this place" if desired.

"We told 'em to go back home," one of the dormitory students said to me. "Whatever cause there is around here, it's ours. They're not really interested in us, just in some other cause."

After May 4, however, the campus found occasion to reflect upon how close we had come to a tragedy of similar proportions. Slowly a germ of truth was leaking out. An anonymous paper (written by one of those who had had early association with the cross burners) was circulated on campus under the heading *The TRUTH*. It appeared June 1, 1970. Near the end of its third page, it noted, "Had everything gone according to plan, Mount Union College and Kent State University would have had a great deal in common."

The dynamics, the give and take of personalities and interests in any gathering of human beings, will always be capable of leading -- and misleading -- the throng. Propagandists have put that knowledge to good use.

I don't really know how close we came to disaster, but I was reminded of the prophetic speech made by Jerry Rubin just 30 days before the Kent State shootings. Speaking on that campus, he said, "Until you people are prepared to kill your parents, you aren't ready for the revolution."

According to the *Boston Herald-Traveler*, Rubin added, "The American school system will be ended in two years. We are going to bring it down. We have to disrupt every institution and break every law."

The *Traveler* editorial at that time noted that Rubin's message to his audience of 1,500 included this statement: "It's quiet here now, but things are going to start again."

They obviously did. Right on schedule.

Rubin's prophecy came true in great measure. In later years the anguish of trials centered on the National Guard and the events of a Saturday morning with tragic deaths of the innocent.

I wonder what Jerry Rubin thought about the sequence.

I wonder how many have pondered the effect of his comments together with the actions of others.

It only takes a few -- one will do -- to bring chaos, given the right chemistry. Back on our campus, after a building takeover failed, there was great concern by a campus segment that the college had tapped the phone lines of the BSU. Otherwise how would the College have stationed Dean DeBow Freed inside Chapman Hall, to appear at 4 a.m., just as militant black students were about to crash open the doors for the takeover? "You will leave, all of you, immediately. Behind every tree around you is a police officer. You will all be arrested if you do not disperse immediately." The Dean was a firm, deliberate man. Authoritative. The students put down their axes and hammers and left.

The Student Life Committee, meeting at 7 that morning in the first floor of the administration building, was interrupted by frantic secretaries who said the president's office was being swarmed by angry students. The Dean of Women, Dean of the College and I left the meeting, hurried to the office and ran into 25 or so white students shouting accusations.

"You tapped the BSU phones!"

"Barbarians! You had no right!"

Nobody seemed to be concerned at all about what would have been smashed doors and windows and total campus disruption.

Dean Debow Freed, stood with grim face, taking all the shouting directed to him. I shall never forget how he simply stood and took it, not arguing or offering return slams. President Ronald Weber wasn't present, having returned home briefly after a night of meetings and watches. Then Terry Taylor, the Dean of Men, came into the office.

"Tapped the phones? You check the phone company. Check the FBI. Check the police. We have *never* tapped any lines."

"Then how did you know the BSU was going to take over Chapman Hall?"

"Yeah. How?"

Dean Freed remained impassive. He offered no explanation.

The scene remains firm in my memory. When I teach creative writing I stress moments of awareness -- those genuine, authentic moments when we realize truths; when you know someone is lying to you, when you know you're going to lose the basketball game, when you know what's inside the letter before you open it. My moment of awareness came after the students finally dispersed -- without explanation on Dean Freed's part. As we resumed our meeting and I was considering some proposals before us, my mind finally caught on to the explanation. The College knew in advance. And it hadn't tapped any lines. And the BSU, goaded by the white liberals, had, indeed, planned strategy at their headquarters -- where their phone was -- to take over the building by force early that morning.

But Dean Freed would not share the explanation.

His grim countenance, his impassive mein was, of course, shielding one lone black student who, in on the discussions, concluded the action was wrong -- and alerted someone "outside" who got the word to Dean Freed. Perhaps that lone student had called the Dean directly -- from another phone.

One person making the difference. Do we realize how much campus life is a melange of actions, from the petty to the momentous? And sometimes one prof can be at the center?

The College meant to do the right thing. I know that the administration meant well when it announced a year following establishment of the Black Students Union in 1970 -- an organization which grew in stature and survived the misdirected actions of a few of its own as well as some white student leaders -- that a bold new plan would bring more blacks to campus. We'd reach out, bring many from the Washington, D.C. area, students who otherwise would not have the chance for experience in a small midwestern, church-related college, probably no college at all. Thirty-one young blacks from Washington were recruited. They came with much fanfare. But they were totally unprepared for our little corner of society. Wayne was one of my favorites. He moved around campus with high-top boots -- and with a knife secreted in a bolster on one of them.

Wayne would use the knife; yes, he pulled it out many times to make a point; after all, recruited from the streets, he was merely continuing the lifestyle he was accustomed to. His language was vicious, his attitude apparently without redeeming factors.

But we got along fine. "Don't shoot!" I'd raise my hands whenever Wayne approached me on campus. "No! No! Not the knife!"

"Oh, I ain't gonna hurt you, Mr. Crist." Wayne would grin, though; and he reveled in the notoriety given him in those brief encounters when I'd dash behind a tree, or kneel in mock despair.

He wanted recognition. Everybody wants recognition. And we all need it. The class valedictorian gets it, so do all those in the honor societies, and the fraternities, and sororities, and those with families to come and applaud and the athletes and so many others.

But the 31 recruits from Washington, D.C., albeit they were objects of some curiosity for a week or so, had little recognition. They were failing courses. By the end of two of our three terms in the academic year, practically all had flunked out; by year's end, none was left. It was not the kind of recognition which boosts anybody's morale.

Wayne lasted just one term.

In retrospect, I have no regrets for my antics. I remember his grin, and his self effacing "I ain't gonna do nuthin" comments. Because when we did our "act" he knew others were watching.

It was about the only recognition Wayne ever had in his brief stay on our campus.

You keep on learning!

On a final examination in American literature class, after ten weeks of good discussion on the philosophies of Emerson, Thoreau, James, Eliot, and others, I tried a twist. I wanted to prod. I wanted an intriguing question. My examination had just one question. And it was one word.

"Why?"

I figured it would be a good way to see how many could respond by citing the various questions raised in the philosophical writings and answering them from the same writings. "Why" appears as a significant dimension in all enduring writings. Why not have the students recall the key questions as well as the answers? Why should I do half their work ! A dangerous approach, but I went ahead with it.

The answers came back in good order; they selected the "why" of self reliance, of higher education, of literary artistry, and of certain life values. Three-fourths through the grading, I had found great similarity in response and my grades were reflecting their similarity.

Then another exam paper was opened, and I found this to be the entire answer:

"Why not?"

And the student had turned in the paper. An unpredictable student, an unpredictable answer -- or was it really? -- and I was confronted with a real test of my own abilities to see questions and answers.

From my desk in the study at home I watched trees bend in a late autumn breeze. I turned down the stereo, walked to the family room where the castle doll house sits. Even the college students, visiting our home each term -- always at least one session for each class -- enjoyed the castle. A bit of fantasy, made for our little daughters, who are now living far from home. Why do I just stand here and let the memories flood? Time sweeps by as clouds passing the face of the moon, occasional gaps giving the only awareness of time. What if there were no gaps at all? But why such thoughts now, when the grade awaits?

A drink of Dr. Pepper now; a nod to my wife (who knows, better than all others, my moods) as I ease back into the study. The stack of other papers, untouched, is mute evidence. A leader of the SDS in 1967 urged in a position paper for that radical group "That the student syndicalist movement adopt as its primary and central issue the abolition of the grade system." I remember, a bit of a smile now. One reason the SDS cited to support their position was that "it is the cause of the alienation of most faculty members from their work."

Fiddlesticks.

Then I put the grade on the paper. An "A."

Some years before, there had been a letter from a wheelchair student who did not return to Mount Union after her initial year. But Larrie Packal was tough and eager for whatever she could do, confined to her wheelchair with stumbled words, and shaking hands. She had written, "Why? Why not? Two questions have been posed and yet for me the latter is the answer. If our lives were as clear and as simple as a pane of glass, what value would they be to us?" She added, "We are not satisfied to dwell among natural pleasures for there is want within every heart, and we seek to obtain."

She wrote these lines:

> Streaks of light are everywhere
> illuminating the spirit of the day.
> Caresses of wind sweep over

projections standing staunchly
upon the ground.
The breeze passes by us -- a trembling sphere --
and whispers: "Try to catch me."

Larrie was right, in so many ways. And the parade of young men and women provide a continuing spirit of self expression of questions and answers and the prof tries to catch them, grasp them, understand them. And the longing within the heart is always for more than mere formal classroom.

I have learned that those of special circumstance have given us the best examples of what academia is supposed to be. Janice Barker, a wheelchair student who was graduated from Mount Union in 1980, writes to me regularly over the years.

She wants "more homework assignments!"

Janice wants to keep on learning, keep on writing poems, keep on writing sketches, keep on sharing experiences.

That is, of course, the best reason to justify English profs... that they might spur others in the individual quests for purpose and achievement.

Sometimes we succeed.

And we learn from each experience.

It happens outside the classroom, of course; the momentary acknowledgements of each other, wispy awareness of common goals. But it is necessarily exaggerated within the classroom.

What is the wind we try to catch?

Adulthood, I suppose. Sometimes it is superficial. Always it is a keeping up with others. Fleeting, monetary values that bend and blow with the very breeze we seek to catch.

The pressures haven't really changed; we still grope for right relationships. The coed dorms have heightened the pressures, I suppose, but the mystique of romance is one of those old reliables for all of us. The flaunt and show of sexual prowess increases -- it's always been a selling job -- and now any night on television and any show, it seems, in the theaters make it more formidable. And we're a bit better in many ways; the arranged marriages of other times were hardly testimonies to our highest achievements.

But they were simpler. I asked a very elderly gentleman in a rest home about his romance of many years gone by.

"I suppose if you could, you would like to live your lifetime over again." It was an inane comment, but it provoked a surprise rejoiner.

"Oh, heavens! Not at all! Why the first time around I found me the right woman. I'd be so scared to go through all that stuff again -- for fear I'd make a mistake and get the wrong one!"

I'm asked if the college students of today are "really that bad" -- that nothing but sex is on their minds. Do all those "terrible things" really go on in the dorms? Some, I'm sure. And they bring the sad statistics of broken homes with them, but I'm no authority. None at all. I wasn't invited to a fraternity house party for endless years. In those earlier campus days of the 1950s and 60s the faculty would chaperon the social parties. Something that went out, I believe, with the Spanish-American war. Why, on one occasion I actually turned in the names of two students involved in a bedroom circumstance which this old prof came upon, quite by accident. I was not invited to a fraternity party for years and years after that time. And we've disposed, anyway, of chaperons many years ago.

I am saddened by the rather mechanical way most students assume what love-making is. How many more mechanical sex manuals will we have? These continue to make money for the authors, so I suppose they will continue as long as we conclude fulfillment of love can be defined by formula. Students today are subjected to so many pressures! I have much sympathy for them. Ironically, in a time in which freedom of expression is so highly touted, so few can find themselves really free. The advice is too overwhelming; they must conform to the myriad of manuals or figure they have missed everything.

I taught three classes when we were on the term system -- 65 students in a ten-week session. During the spring term in 1982, I had one abortion and three unwed fathers in my classes. The girl who aborted her child did not tell me; her roommate did. The unmarried fathers, however, each came to me with requests for absence from campus for "a few days." Each explained the circumstance. The first two were merely "going home" for a while to "supervise" things.

But when Bob came to the office with his request, the old English prof exploded. I shouted a bit, told him he was a disgrace, that he hadn't the first idea what responsibility meant. Oh, I put on quite a show -- until the boy shrank to the floor and began to cry.

I quickly got up, shut the office door, and put my arms around him. "Look, I forgot something."

He continued sobbing. I said, "We're both human beings."

Fifteen minutes later we were still on the floor, now going over his plans. He had said, "I'm going home to marry her."

"Then take the time from class. I'll work with you when you get back. We can make up the tests."

Four out of the 65 students in my classes -- four that I knew of. How many more in a typical semester?

But there was one who was willing to assume responsibility.

Views from the prof who had at that time been teaching for 30 years. The *Dynamo*, campus paper, probably had my type in mind in a recent issue when a columnist noted that something he'd like to see would be a "prof talk about the partying and loose morals on campus without sounding jealous!"

Love has so many ways of expression -- or lack of it. In class the young woman was bright, motivated, and attractive. And married. It was the attitude of her husband which led to my getting to know her better.

After missing class several days, she came in, sat in the back, strangely aloof. Her right eye was swollen. Again, another day missed, and she then was back, trying to be alone. Her face puffed up. I mentioned her absences, something not like her usual pattern.

Then came the story of her almost regular pattern of being beaten by her husband. "I love him, I really do. He doesn't mean it. It's his temper."

We went on as usual until my phone rang at home -- at 5 a.m. -- some weeks later. She was crying. Marilyn and I went to her that morning; we found her swollen, crying, hurting on a street corner. Later we got the student and her husband to visit the campus psychologist -- and found out the root of the problem. Her husband, who insisted that he loved the girl, was merely following a pattern given him years before. From rural mid-southern stock, he had seen his dad regularly beat his mother, part of a "routine," an accepted pattern of male domination. Nourished on such action, he transferred it to his own wife, regularly asserting his authority while at all other times showing compassion and sharing.

But idealism remains. For me, for others. Misguided perhaps, but still there. Susie married her high school sweetheart, but found the marriage floundering after several years. Writing to me of her idealism, she said, "I thought love would just be walking along the beach, watching sunsets, holding hands, and just being together." Ah! Those grade "C" movies!

I wrote her, "You are finding that sometimes your feet hurt on the hard shell edges as you walk along that beach and sometimes clouds hide the sunset glow, and sometimes hands hang limp, and sometimes being together you are finding yourself strangely alone."

Nobody *makes* love. The phrase is a blot on both language and humanity. Love cannot be manufactured as pots and pans; that is precisely its dilemma -- and its greatness.

But I preach too much. That is a failing of some English professors: they expect the class to be assembled, listening to every sparkling word, fascinated as they capture the beauties of literature, explain the complexities of grammar -- and then assume to preach of all human behavior.

"Literature" has many meanings. Frankly, I think my student who wrote in her journal the following statement back in the mid-1960s probably captured a sentiment about love as well as anyone has ever done -- though the statement may have insignificant "literary" appeal to most:

"I want to be proposed to after I've had the flu three days, just thrown up, in my non-fitting pinned flannel pajamas, clumped hair and oily nose... I know our love would last."

Beautiful!

Literature and current social dilemmas *are* tied together, but it is too easy for me (and perhaps there are others) to take advantage of that classroom situation, the captive audience to preach our social views. What is most needed is to live those views, live them openly and unashamedly.

It is the living that brings to each of us the insights and values which, in turn, provide the tools for teaching. If I ask students what the world was like when they were born, any response is at best second-hand. Yet I know something of what it was like. And they say, "How old are you now?" When I was 38, some guessed "at least 50."

"Oh, I can't be that old." Then I lean back. "It was just yesterday when it was the sixth inning at the park and I was pitching and staring in the catcher's mitt. If he wiggled three fingers that meant a curve ball; if he wiggled five fingers it meant a spitter; if he held out his fist that meant my slow ball -- and it really didn't matter what he wiggled for all my pitches were the same. But I'm sure that was just yesterday."

Students snicker a bit, not really meaning to be impolite, but the white beard today, sparse hair, the face lines betray. Still, it's hard to be calm when the prof indulges himself. "You're old," they say.

"We know you always use the elevator in Chapman Hall. And you've been married an awful long time."

One says, "I guess your marriage worked, huh? And that's why you think all of us should follow tradition, huh? I mean, like getting married and stuff."

A girl asks, "How do you know when you really love somebody?"

I can only respond in light of my own experience. That is all a prof can do with Mark Twain or the mass media or poetic theory.

"When did you know you were in love? Was there a moment of awareness, like you talk about in creative writing class?"

I say, "One day I was crying and this young woman touched my hand and by touching it I knew it mattered to her and when she did that I did not cry any more."

The phrasing surprises them. "You mean with tears down your cheek?" One asks, "Were you in an accident?"

"No. I showed no tears at all."

"But you told us you were crying."

Indeed I was, but it was all inside, without tears, without sound.

A brief snicker now. One says, "Then how did she know you were crying?" Look of triumph on the student now. "How did she know if there were no tears at all?"

I said, "Ah, my students, that is precisely what love is."

6

Relations with the Public

Mary Ekey, rest her soul, was a ponderous grade school teacher whose voice demanded absolute obedience. If there was any doubt, she reinforced it with the rod -- and no courtroom ever challenged her.

Donald Kerr sat in front of me in the first row, grade seven at South Lincoln school. And Mary Ekey had cause, she concluded, to give him a clout on this particular winter morning. She grabbed the rod from the chalk board, strode with vengeance to him, and swung mightily. Unfortunately, her aim was not as precise as her anger. The rod in a mighty arc crashed into the back of my head, caromed, and finally found its mark. For good measure, to impress Don further, she did follow through with a second whack -- from the side. I somehow survived despite the blow.

At lunch time classes were dismissed for the trek home. Apparently Don mentioned something of the confrontation to his mother at that time, for halfway into the afternoon session, Mrs. Kerr came to the classroom door and engaged in lively discussion. "My boy..." and "...struck him!" as well as other snatches of the conversation drifted into my awareness.

Then I heard Miss Ekey say, "All right! I'll just show you that it was not that bad. I'll show you how I did hit him." With this she picked up the rod, came over to our row to whack poor Donald one more time. I should have known. Miss Ekey disciplinarian and knew her subject matter. But a .400 h not.

Another mighty swing, another wide arc as Mrs. Kerr watched in horror -- and another blow to the wrong head. I was clobbered by mistake for a second time. "What about the role of the disciplinarian in the classroom?" Professional education groups ask this question of the olde prof many times.

"Well... I'm not sure about physical punishment, but if you must, make sure your aim is just as good as your lofty ideals!"

Miss Ekey had reason, I suppose, for trying to clobber poor Donald. And even in today's liberal society it might hold up in court. All of which illustrates how matters have changed. Back in the 17th century, one Henry Peacham in his essay *The Complete Gentleman* wrote that he knew of one schoolmaster "who in Winter would ordinarily in a cold morning whip his Boyes over for no other purpose than to get himself in a heat."

I have not reached that valley of behavior, however sustaining it might seem; not for discipline nor for body heat have I exercised myself that way in class. Never aimed a paddle. In fact, there are times it's been clear I never even knew how to aim!

Consider the eighth grade, in those salad years when grade school principals were both administrators and teachers. William Cobb was a demanding fellow at South Lincoln, disciplining by the seat of its pants. He also would select the first boy in the first row of his eighth grade assembly room to be the appointed tardy-alarm ringer.

The bell, located behind an ancient Victrola, was at the landing, top of the second floor stairs. At the beginning of my eighth grade year, I reported, as did all others, to the home room of the previous year; then, on signal, we moved to our new classroom. At that point, I wanted more than all else to get the coveted first seat. I ran. I pushed, I shoved.

But Gilbert got there first. I was behind him, assigned to the second seat in the first row. I kept wishing he would get sick, take a trip to Florida -- anything, but just be absent! However, on he went, duly appointed keeper of the bells -- and player of the John Philip Sousa record which provided the tempo for our orderly march out of school each afternoon.

Then the great day came; Gilbert didn't make it to school. Mr. Cobb stared at me at precisely 8 a.m. that fated day, then made a cursory nod, saying, "Lyle -- you may go out and ring the tardy bell now!"

Never before had I received such a glorious message! I dashed into the hallway, chest swelling with pride and accomplishment, ran past the Victrola, reached up for the chain hanging on the wall, the chain which I had passed everyday for years, the chain which activated the tardy bell located high above the Victrola -- and only then, in that magical moment of awareness, did I notice that there were *two* such chains, and I did not know which one to pull to ring the tardy bell. The debate lasted just seconds; then I pulled one of the chains.

It was the earliest fire drill in the history of South Lincoln school.

After all, a fire drill bell is never activated unless it's just before lunch time or just before afternoon dismissal. And even then you see the Chief's truck parked outside, and red-suited men in the halls prior to the drill.

But at 8 a.m. this alarm had to be for real! Panic followed -- kids running, teachers screaming after their broods. Hallways filled immediately with chaos. Somehow through the screaming hordes, Mr. Cobb managed to reach me, still standing by the Victrola, trying to comprehend the full impact of my disastrous choice of chains.

"Lyle! Lyle!" His voice strained above the din. "What will we do now?"

There appeared only one positive step for me to suggest. Responding in equally shrill tones, I gulped, "I could start playing John Philip Sousa!"

It might have been better if I had thrown a match into the Victrola. We could have justified the commotion throughout the entire neighborhood.

Some of us never get the classroom -- and its concomitant bells, rods, and phonographs -- out of our systems. For me, it's been a lifetime of education -- in the formal sense. From grade school through high school, from undergraduate to graduate universities and then into teaching, from all this the atmosphere has not been the commercial marketplace. After Purdue I did remain in research briefly, working on technical reports tied in with the wind tunnel there.

Then it was trade journal writing for a while. Learning to write up new products, telling stories of how somebody achieved success in the plumbing business, in furniture, in promotion of clay products, in iron and steel. Formula writing, actually, but an excellent discipline to learn. Of course, there may be something said for not learning too quickly, too.

Take the very first article I ever had accepted for publication. I was still a senior at Purdue. Keep in mind now that I was probably the only guy at Purdue who preferred writing up the lab reports to doing the technical analysis, the measurement, lab set-ups, etc. I was the philosopher and writer, apparently.

Early in that senior year I wrote "A Philosophy for Engineers," posing the question -- from Aristotle -- of whether engineers deliberate sufficiently over their decision makings. I probed the versatility of technical approaches, the engineer's contribution to community life, and our desire to inform ourselves of all matters profound, materially and spiritually. I incorporated a specific instance of bridge design resulting from an objective rather than subjective analysis of the challenge by a British designer. I even used the word "behooves," which certainly is the mark of a deep and long-time thinker.

At least the editors of *Trained Men* magazine must have thought so. The nationally-circulated publication for education not only sent me a check for $15 in payment for the goodies in the article but also asked for a complete "resume of my technical and engineering experience." That would be used to inform their readers of the broad background and expertise from which my golden words came.

"What'll I do?" My question was directed at my roommate, who was a far better engineering student than I'd ever be.

"You might tell them the truth."

"But then they'd want their $15 back!" After all, this was my very first accepted-for-publication writing other than the high school and campus newspapers.

My next writing exercise was even more difficult than "A Philosophy for Engineers." I had to give the editors magnificent technical background and yet remain truthful. Not an easy task.

I had helped my brother put in a sidewalk the previous summer. The year before that I operated the elevator at the City Savings Bank and Trust Building at home.

"My experience," I wrote the editors, "includes supervision of roadway development. In addition, I have worked closely with the financial aspects of transportation, though one might say that my career with them had its ups and downs."

I framed the $15 check. For a month or so. Then I used it to buy textbooks for the winter semester.

Trained Men bought a second article from me two years later. It was titled "English and the Technical Man."

Fortunately, they did not ask for an update at that time on either my highway or my financial activities.

Since those days I've been in education in one form or another. The "other" includes five years as director of public relations for

Mount Union College. That was a learning time, too -- and not without its own brand of problems. Three cited now should be sufficient.

I was on the gridiron sidelines next to the coach, eagerly awaiting a touchdown which would enable me to write "The Raiders put on a strong finish, closing the gap on Baldwin-Wallace College with a TD in the waning moments." Or something equally positive.

I would ignore the fact that Baldwin-Wallace was ahead 38-0 up to that point. PR writers stress only the positive. Fourth down, two yards to go. If we could make those yards, we'd have a minute or so left, keep possession of the ball inside the opposition's ten-yard line, and perhaps achieve that touchdown. Coach Bully Jones put his hand on the padded shoulders of a substitute tackle and muttered a play to him. I did not catch the full conversation, but it must have been something like "Have Dave call a 77-H."

In hustled the left tackle. The message was given to the quarterback, though, in retrospect, I assume a bit garbled in the confusion. The quarterback -- a third-stringer, put in when all else was lost -- squatted, called magic signals, and the teams lined up for the big moment. The coach edged forward. The bench edged forward. I edged forward.

On the field the Purple Raiders edged forward, but at the snap of the ball, it appeared that everyone, including the backfield, stopped edging and turned around for a look at what would happen next. Chaos. Dave didn't want the ball, tried to hand if off to several others, each of whom hesitated, as though contemplating the late movie, then declined with thanks. Nobody wanted the ball but by the time a quorum could be gathered for further discussion, the quarterback was swamped -- six yards behind the line of scrimmage. I'd have to think up a new headline for my story.

Saddened, the team trooped from the field, the defensive unit going in for the final minute. The coach reached out for the young quarterback. "My God!" the coach cried, "What a goof up out there! What play did you call?"

"A 57-H is what I thought it was."

"57-H? My God, we don't even have a play with that number!"

Dave looked straight ahead. "I didn't think we did either."

Miss Ekey would have been proud of that boy. He knew never to raise questions.

The quarterback's mix-up was no worse than mine the next season, determined as I was to put dear old Mount Union on the map through stellar public relations tactics. Attendance was down at our games; I wanted to enliven things. I arranged for a lightplane to swoop over the field exactly at 2 p.m. on Saturday, just as the game against Ohio Wesleyan would be getting underway. I'd have cheerleaders ready -- and the game ball would be dropped from the plane, caught by the cheerleaders -- and on with the contest! Now, that would bring the watchers, make headlines for the vaunted Purple and White!

Well, not exactly. At the magic hour the plane did swoop -- but dropped no football. Afterwards I called the airport.

"Yeah, we were there. But when we swooped over the field there wasn't nobody around. I didn't even see no spectators, so I flew on."

The fact that one grandstand had a roof explained things. Partly. The fact that there were so few in the other stand and that my cheerleaders were idly watching from the sidelines, having forgotten instructions, added to the problem.

I did not receive the Public Relations Society of America Award that year for meritorious service.

Conditions just did not seem right for me to achieve an excellent name in public relations work on our campus. Take the case of the celebrated senior-alumni boat race.

To help matters on the annual alumni day, I suggested we have a gala rowboat race on the campus lakes -- a blending of two relatively shallow dredged-out areas which served as focal point for springtime romances. The custom, according to long-held tradition, was that students becoming engaged would stroll to the narrow wooden bridge straddling the watery areas and pledge their troths. This apparently worked well except for almost-yearly sabotaging of the bridge, with assorted fires wrecking havoc with its slats, if not the amorous couples.

"It's a great idea," the alumni secretary told me. And so we planned the boat race. I visioned the competing squads of four seniors and four well-chosen alumni paddling with fervor across the lakes, waving in loyal memories to those gathered on the bridge -- and leading to a rousing finish on the other side mid cheers of boosters.

We had the boats. Seniors picked their crew; that memorable morning the alumni did, too. Crowds roared and they were off.

"Go, go!"

"Mush! Mush!"

There are some factors which, in retrospect, become quite logical. For one, the alumni men had put on a few more pounds --

and it showed -- not across their waists as much as in the posture of their rowboat.

"Go! Go!"

"It ain't going!"

"Look! The alums are stuck!"

They were. Right in the middle of our massive lake. About where the depth was 30 inches or so. Their boat, thoroughly mired, was first the object of awe, then laughter -- and finally some concern.

"Man, it's quicksand!"

I had visions of the Associated Press wire headlining the story "Four Alumni Lose Lives as Result of PR Man's Stunt." Or others to that effect. Fortunately, the seniors -- now across the lake and clearly the victors -- jumped out of their boat and waddled to the rescue. There was no quicksand. Just red faces. And muddy bodies.

I found it appropriate to suggest the College consider dredging the lakes in the near future. After all, we might lose fish, too, in the mire.

Or lovers. Especially if they would include a baptism ritual while pledging their troths.

But all other events pale before what was to become known as "Crist's Disaster" in 1959. Still determined to bring the very best in spectacle sports to our little college and its loyal band of rooters, I staged a gala bicycle race at halftime of a Saturday night football contest. The five campus fraternities and the independents were enthusiastic. They practiced all week on the cinder oval which surrounded the playing field. Anticipation was at the traditional fever pitch. My advance news stories were classics of magnetic attraction. The stands were almost full.

The first half of the game ended, and the opponent's band took to the field. I had not planned on that band showing up -- unfortunately -- but their program was fairly brief and pleasant. The cyclists were touring up and down the track in front of the closed stands, revving engines. Then our band took to the field, about ten minutes behind my planned schedule. The cyclists rippled muscles and greased chains for their big moment.

"This will be the highlight of the season," I confided to a colleague. "We will make headlines all over northeastern Ohio." Prophetic words.

Finally our band snaked off the field. Twelve cyclists lined up at the starting line, the 50-yard line in front of the covered stands. The teams were in their locker rooms under the open stands across the way. "Gentlemen," I said to the cyclists, "start your engines!"

Into the first turn we lost two bikers, skidding on the loose cinders. Blood ran. I flinched, but knew that the one-lap race would be a thriller nonetheless. Into the full turn, sideliners cheering wildly. The cyclists were bunched, no one in full command. Exciting! Then out of that first turn, still bunched, starting to head down the straightway in front of the open stands, gathering more speed, still bunched, the cheering, the roaring of the crowd. A PR man's dream!

Then it happened.

At full tilt, just as the cyclists neared the tunnel opening from the locker rooms, the vaunted Purple Raider gridders, buoyed by a classic halftime talk, on sharp edge to turn the tide of the game, did its own roaring out of the tunnel. I could see it all coming, even from across the field. The ends, tackles, halfbacks -- everybody on the team -- dashed from the tunnel, crossing the cinder oval just as the speeding cyclists, still bunched, headed toward them at ninety degrees.

People still talk about it today. Protest riots, confrontations, invective shoutings, building takeovers -- nothing of the late 1960s could match the mayhem of that collision of the late 1950s. The two bikers who had fallen in the turn were remembered as being the least injured. I was remembered for not having remembered to have somebody there to hold the team back at halftime.

I worked on headlines a long time that night.

But nothing seemed to come out right enough to submit to the Public Relations Society for award consideration that year either.

7

Bonehead Composition

Many moons ago I sent a note to the chairman of the English Department regarding the selection of textbooks for the basic writing course. I noted the alliterative approach to many titles: *Contexts for Composition, Subject and Structure, Paragraphs in Prose, Sense and Sentences* being among the long-time favorites. All of this could lead to something like *Pronouns in Profile* or *Modifiers, Moods, and Meanings*. I thought that something like *Participles I Have Dangled* might also be effective, using a very personal approach. On the other hand, we might consider a narrative angle and adopt a book with a title like *The Adventures Of Pat Prose, Boy Essayist*.

But all of these are by the boards now. In that long span of teaching years, new vistas have opened. If I were to concoct a similarly whimsical note for my current chair I'd consider the Apollo age we've been in -- and encourage publishers to come up with texts carrying titles such as *Countdown to Composition* or the *Space Age Style Book*. How about *Rhetoric for Robots*? There is an implication there, of course, which may be truer than one wishes.

Capturing the no-nonsense spelling of the era and combining it with the space age we might find *From Kape Kennedy to Kareful Komposition*.

Finally, I'm sure some students would appreciate a text titled *Into Orbit with Theme Writing*. *Scientific Grammar* does have some merit, but better would be *Blasting Off to Better Themes*.

For cover design we might look for a silver Gemini nose cone puncturing a sky-blue paragraph and a neat sub-title as follows: *Super-Sonic Sentences for Sub-Sonic Minds.*

Again, there's an implication which disturbs me a bit. The problem is that the minds referred to might, on occasion, be those of the profs!

The teaching of writing is the kind of occupation which has built-in opportunities for profs to ignore goals -- all except getting out to the golf course by 10 a.m. I saw the entire writing output of a student who had taken freshman English, the basic writing course, at a large state university in Ohio.

Four papers. A total of eight typewritten pages.

Four fictional accounts. In the entire course there was not a single assignment to write information, to give explanation, to develop one persuasive essay. Instead, just four brief fictionalized "accounts." For an entire semester.

"We were supposed to be strong on description," the young woman told me.

And I'm strong on reaction. Four papers, each graded by a graduate student, each carrying the mark of A. Not one paper had a mark, a correction, a compliment, a comment of any kind by the grader or the prof.

"He just taught this one course," she told me.

"What did you do in the class?"

"We read assignments he gave us from a book of readings."

"You read them?"

"Aloud. We were called on to read for five minutes or so. When you weren't reading you were asleep."

No matter that even a cursory reading showed a half dozen spelling errors, several dangling participles, with hackneyed phrases all over the place. Grading must, I know, be more than picking out errors. "Did you ever have conferences with the prof about your writing?"

"Never."

After a golf match near Akron, Ohio, recently, we stopped in a local establishment; while the others were chatting and celebrating their victory -- I shoot 98 every time I play, regardless of my frequency on the course -- I took out my sorrows in conversation with the young man behind the counter. By no surprise, he found out I was an English prof.

"I had an English prof last year. Really liked her. We talked about sex and politics and social things, you know what I mean? It was like we really had a great time."

"Freshman English?"

"Composition. Like she was really neat, you know?"

"How many papers did you write?"

"I didn't write no papers. I mean, like, we just talked. Know what I mean?"

"She was a good prof?"

"Like I really agreed with everything she said. You know?"

Well, if I didn't at least I found out what makes a good prof. I must work on tolerance. For all these years I've been urging avoidance of the double negative and stuff like that, you know what I mean? Later, I checked out the catalog where the young man had attended. Checked the course he had completed. It was called "Basic Composition."

You and I can spend a semester talking about how to cut the grass in the front yard -- or parallel north and south lines, diagonally perhaps -- or maybe going around the trees and widening the circles. And we can talk about the height of the blade, lubrication, how to hold the handle of the power mower. But we'll never get the lawn mowed until we begin pushing the mower out, guiding it -- cutting. I rather think learning to write is the same process we have to do more than merely talk. Even if we are in agreement on sex and politics -- and stuff. Sometimes that basic course is referred to as "Bonehead Comp." A nasty term, but used -- especially by upperclassmen. Richard Armour, the witty poet, has suggested that the term be dropped by all of us, even from light-hearted conversation. He says, "I think it is unfortunate to refer, even playfully, to 'bonehead English.' For one thing, I am not sure who are the boneheads. The students? The professors, many of whom are atrocious writers?"

In the case of my young friend who had not been required to write at all in a basic writing course, the term might well apply to those who do not teach. Writing courses, I need note, have never really been in great vogue.

Writing in *The New York Times*, Ronald Berman points to the decline in composition courses on campuses, saying, "the remedial class is a kind of Sunday School on campus."

We do like to talk about it, though. Participating in professional writers' conferences regularly, I have opportunity to note familiar faces of those who come yearly to ask about writing, to listen to writers discuss their trade, to analyze and criticize -- but who never attempt to write. These older adults in a way typify some college students who profess great need for and interest in writing skills, but who lack the incentive to move them into the process.

Why learn to write at all? I like Berman's point: "One never knows what he knows until it is written." W. H. Auden said essentially the same thing. Lewis Carroll once noted that the hardest activity in the world is to be original. Original thinking, translated into words on paper, offers witness to perhaps the highest human achievements.

There are some 650,000 words out there in the English language. A typical issue of *The New York Times* may use 150,000 of them. Writing is a process of selection and rejection; we select the words from our working vocabulary to express our ideas, and we reject the words which do not fit. That's the best reason in the world, of course, for teaching and developing vocabulary: without a suitable reservoir of words, we'll never be making any selection, certainly not making any rejections. We'll just be using the same few words over and over again -- like, you know what I mean?

My phrasing may be simpler, but I think it's getting at the same conclusion Berman does when he uses a loftier phrase to summarize the process of writing: "A series of conceptual decisions."

I'd better be careful how I use his phrasing in class. I'll probably get some snickers -- and a theme on why we should have coed dorms.

Leonardo DiVinci pondered the process of writing, concluding that poets are nothing more than traders -- they borrow a bit from this person, a bit from that person, then assemble the words and ideas from all sources into their own "original" efforts. Again, the borrowing -- whether one agrees fully with DiVinci -- always goes back to the 650,000 raw words we must all begin with.

We do think in terms of concepts, we use the words manifesting the concepts which show our decisions. This English prof says to have the decisions involves specifics, images. We write because we have something popping around in our minds which we want to share; people will grasp the decisions if they are given in pictures.

When *Star Wars* became so popular, a TV commercial showed a set of toy figures from the movie. The toys had not yet been manufactured, would not be in the stores for some months; what was being sold, according to a news story, was a "gift package" -- a certificate to claim the products later. Camera work dramatized the toys and at the same time a voice explained to viewers that the toys were not yet available.

Was the voice heard? A survey showed that viewers almost unanimously remembered the pictures, ignored the spoken words.

We prefer pictures; that's why the writer, the student, needs to be taught to use picture words.

Regardless of your views on trapping, you will grasp the significance of one former trapper's viewpoint in this brief poem:

> Somewhere
> in the dim beyond
> three muskrats wait for me.
>
> Accusingly
> they hold up stumps
> of legs chewed free from traps.
>
> Freedom
> and life are worth
> whatever the sacrifice.
>
> They
> keep telling me
> over and over and over again.

Evan Lodge, a Mount Union graduate and retired English teacher, gave us this one significant picture. How much better than hecatombs of borrowed, long-winded phrases!

Knowing this, many students ask, then why learn all that gunk about parts of speech? That stuff went out with the Hupmobile and took diagramming with it. Some of the profs can remember those "good old days" of learning sentence structure. Can you imagine anybody having to go through that torture in this enlightened age?

Never mind; we'll get a new approach. "Systematic sentence analysis" or "interpretive sentence adjuncts" will help. The names mean nothing, of course, but they ease the pain a bit. Well, I'll try them. As soon as I figure out what they mean. One of my many weaknesses is that I'm not quite sophisticated enough to understand much of educational jargon. I got off on the wrong track about a decade ago when, in a moment of severe guilt complex (just returned from a National Council of Teachers of English meeting), I decided to improve my professional reading, plunging into a 40-page monograph of the teaching of writing. The fellow who wrote the article knew far more about linguistic theory than I ever will, but it was a dark and cloudy event for me.

In all the 40 pages, the professor never used the word "writing." Every time that word was called for, the professor used a more sophisticated phrasing -- he called it the "scribal act."

The more I think about it, the dirtier it sounds!

I don't know why he just didn't say "writing."

Another prof has referred to poor writing as "scribblestutter." Now, *that's* a worthy phrase!

Encounters such as these lead me to conclude that some basics are not all that bad. Even parts of speech and diagramming. Come to think of it, "parts of speech" could become "componential elements of interpersonal communication." With that as a starter just think what we can do with "diagramming;" "photostructural representation." Or "scribal elucidation." Look at all the progress we've made!

And here I am in freshman English class suggesting to this tall, lean young man that he should sharpen his vocabulary. "Trouble with this paper, Ron, is that you use too many generalizations. For instance you say "The world is involved with many things." Sharpen that! Specify! I go to the brownboard and write down the five S's of good writing:

Subordination
Summary
Series
Sequence

...and, with a flair, I dash off the final one: Specifics.

"This is an easy way to think of my guidelines. All begin with 'S.' "

Such a mode of recall -- all beginning with the same letter -- is called a "mnemonic." I was never sure how to pronounce that term -- had a bit of scribblestutter, perhaps; wisely, I refrain from dwelling on the technical aspects. I slurred the word "mnemonics" -- you get good at doing this after ten or twelve years -- and smiled. The class hastened to their pencils, putting the list in their notebook pages. Rod nodded, understanding. He promised to be more specific next time.

Next time occurred the following Wednesday when theme #6 came in. The topic had something to do with personal judgment in a time of crisis. Such a crisis developed, alas, when I read Ron's paper in the office that afternoon. Ron wanted to say, "Then I had an idea." That is what he should have said. However, remembering the call to the specifics, he apparently had gone to the dictionary to trump up each term into something "better."

The line now read: "Another aspect of the dilemma emigrated into my pate."

The dilemma was mine now -- and certain aspects were emigrating; I watched them trek across the desk waiting for the next boat. On Thursday I called Ron aside. "What in the dickens is this sentence? Why didn't you just say you had an idea?"

His eyes brightened. "You can't fool me, Prof. Crist. I knew you wanted lots of them words. This is more specific, right?"

Dark clouds are gathering around Chapman Hall. "Well, there's a difference between one's pate and one's mind."

"Well, the dictionary said 'pate' was 'head.' "

Birds are hurrying for places of refuge from the storm. Thunder is heard. "There is a difference between one's head and one's mind."

"Well, you didn't talk about that." Ron was triumphant in defense.

I write this 20 years later, because today my notes call for clarification of "pate" and "mind" in all my classes.

But perhaps I did not talk sufficiently of what might be termed priorities in dealing with another freshman paper. My good friend Joe was great on baseball, but had not really made the distinction between a noun and a pronoun by the time he was accepted at Mount Union. The research paper is to be the magnum opus of English 100, the final paper, the most demanding. Joe's library research paper, a classic in confusion, was on the obviously scholarly topic of "Babe Ruth: Baseball Hero." I do not think it is entirely television's fault that Joe wrote, "Babe married Claire Hodgeson in April 17, 1929 at five o'clock in the morning. He was 90 for 136 the rest of the season..."

One hundred and thirty six what? I should check with Mrs. Ruth, of course. Well, so be it. Joe's interests in specifics was commendable. We find that Babe was married at 5 a.m. -- but are not quite sure why (though he did have a .625 average for something) -- and at the end of the paper we find "On the night of August 17 he died at approximately 8:01."

That, I submit, is solid research. And, for all its dilemmas, it's about two stories above the note I received from a disgruntled freshman several years before. He wrote, "I really get pised off when I think how low you grade me..."

Spelling, of course, is not the end product, but our highest goal. In fact, misspellings sometimes are great revelators of hidden circumstances. I recall the freshman who got mixed up in his terminology, writing that he felt bad, but saying "I am in the debts of depression."

I was in the "debts" as well, come to think of it, when a young woman, speaking of the distinctive career of Susan B. Anthony, wrote, "She was a very unique person -- especially during the time in which she lived." I can't think of a better time to be unique. Or even *very* unique -- even though that is a linguistic impossibility.

Some specific incident from Anthony's life would have helped give the picture. It's always pictures. Always anecdotes and examples. It's taken me a quarter century to realize that simple fact. One of the 52 hostages in Iran said, "There was fear so strong you could feel it vibrating in the air... there was a hollow feeling that you are a shadow on the wall and you keep getting smaller as the sun goes down and you pray the sun never really goes away."

That rates an "A" in my book.

Grades stem from grammar in English, drills again and again, work on spelling, work on punctuation, work on avoiding confusing of "further" and "farther" (there are rules) or "good" and "well" (there are clear, specific rules).

Yet those "rules" break down in the minds of some authors.

It was Gertrude Stein (who certainly became far better known than I!) who said, for instance, of the comma: "A comma by helping you along holding your coat for you and putting on your shoes keeps you from living your life as actively as you should lead it and to me for many years and I still feel that way about it only now I do not pay as much attention to them..."

I get a kick out of her further observation: "At most a comma is a poor period that lets you stop and take a breath but if you want a breath you ought to know yourself that you want to take a breath..."

Maybe if we do write correctly (beyond the rules?) there would be no need for the comma. Is that possibly blasphemy? Are rules the key to good writing? Jim Quinn writes excellent satire -- and also makes some points regarding rules. He detests what he calls "yahoo pop grammarians" who dwell solely on the rules, and forget that language changes.

"Pop grammarians," teachers of bonehead composition, businessmen who can't find secretaries who know the difference between "stationery" and "stationary" and Monday morning copy editors of Sunday papers -- these he refers to as "jot and tittle experts." Their solution is simple -- back to the basics.

I agree about a too-strict perhaps blind adherence to the basics, yet I cannot ignore them, when I read that police picked up the driver who was "driving in an erotic fashion" on the highway -- or the man picked up for "uttering and threathening." I'm curious about erotic road patterns and I do not understand why threathening (whatever it is) is a crime.

I pondered much over my role in teaching.

I think of the young lady in my American literature class in 1983. "Why do we have to read this stuff? I liked some of the stories earlier in the semester, but this gunk is so difficult!"

We had been probing Melville's "Benito Cereno." Long paragraphs, lots of symbols, long sentences, and chock full of stream-of-consciousness phrasings. "Rip Van Winkle" was enjoyable (and undoubtedly discussed in high school), but this was beyond the limits!

Back to the basics? Are there legitimate long sentences, difficult phrasings, paragraphs? Should integral calculus be as simple as seventh grade arithmetic? Should we merely keep on studying the multiplication tables instead of probing other aspects of math? Will the spectator role which television and VCRs have placed on so many people eliminate the need for deeper thought and appreciation?

I am hesitant to answer. Yet the spelling, the subordination, the series -- and the specifics persist from my point of view.

And back two hundred years ago there was a gentleman who knew how to use specifics, the picture words of writing. Benjamin Franklin was our first poet, short story writer, and novelist -- even though he wrote none of these. He wrote letters -- and an autobiography -- and political statements which made wonderful use of specifics. The story is told of a pending action by Congress which would limit voting to only those persons who owned property. Many were upset at this thought; they drafted a petition of concern which reads like something from a law school paper, but totally lacking in pictures:

> It cannot be adhered to with any reasonable
> degree of intellectual or moral certainty that the inalienable

right man possesses to exercise his political preferences by employing his vote in referendums is rooted in anything other than man's own nature, and is, therefore, properly called a natural right. To hold, for instance, that this natural right can be limited externally by making its exercise dependent upon a prior condition of ownership of property is to wrongly suppose that man's natural right to vote is somehow more inherent in and dependent on the property of man than it is on the nature of man. It is obvious that such belief is unreasonable, but it reverses the order of rights intended by nature.

They showed the petition, sounding as though it had been formulated by a committee of attorneys, to Franklin, who said it would not convince anybody. He offered to rewrite the petition. His version says just about all a prof can say regarding the value of picture words:

> To require property of voters leads us to this dilemma: I own a jackass, I can vote. The jackass dies; I cannot vote. Therefore my vote represents not me but the jackass.

Further, Franklin's selection of references (just as we select and reject individual words from that vocabulary) is beautiful: what politician would ever want to admit that he had been swept into office by the vote of a group of jackasses?

But profs need to remember that not all students come out of the Franklin mold. Nor do the profs. I'm in awe rather than fascination at the computers which spew out names, dates, entrance indexes. The machines so easily present me with students in alphabetical order, test scores, social security numbers -- whatever is needed; whatever except the hearts and souls represented by those data. If I had 7,000 freshmen taking writing courses I'd probably view all the statistical miracles very positively, but the danger remains in the automating of the minds. Students can too easily be pawns in a huge numbers game. Pre-classroom categorizing can go too far. The temptation is to check the board scores, note the neat columns, and go ahead, put the final grade in the book, stereotype the students, and so what is there to teaching?

For this English prof there was a better way. Write something for the prof. Response to a couple of good essay questions will reveal all I really need to know about achievement, vocabulary, intelligence.

Better, it will tell me about the student's ability -- and willingness -- to pick up all the essentials, toss them in a useful package, and hand it to me. Seldom do young people get the chance to loft their views to a listening older person -- but it's my job to listen. What they say is more important than any statistical norm, poll or academic study. Statistics never show personality. A paragraph can do that. Vocabulary can do that.

One student showed his interest in the wilderness by using the wilderness as his frame of reference -- he showed his fascination when he wrote of a lone heron "stilting through the bog." Marvelous verb! Capturing the picture, moving the action, conveying the penetrating mind of the young writer.

Everybody has something worthwhile to say; if we can get the words to do justice to what is inside, we will have our measure of achievement. All I need at first is the degree of proficiency in the expression; I'll get as well some measure of depth of thought. The difficulty -- and opportunity -- is providing the situation, the motivation for my students to want to open up.

John was taking a test from me in the 1970s, but wrote the following instead of answering my questions:

> ...you said just to be yourself, so I will lay it out to you the best I can. I find this test to be very interesting and of no extreme difficulty -- it is a test I would have enjoyed taking had I been better prepared and mentally ready. But at the moment I am not in the proper frame of mind to accept the challenge offered by this test.

I'm saying to myself, "He's copping out, trying to worm his way out of the test. Look at the lofty phrasing so far." He continues:

> Perhaps it is not important why I am in this perplexed state of mind. I really don't know if it is or not. What is important is what I am doing about this state of mind. What I choose to do is take an 'F' instead of the other alternatives. Don't get me wrong, I did not come into this test cold! However, I can not take it. No,

> I would not have gotten an "A" but what is in my head is all jumbled and refuses to come out.
> If I could only capture my sentiment with this ink perhaps you could better understand the choice I have made. But the best I can do is just to say I feel of another time and of another place.

I'm telling myself, "He will never get to the reason. He has no *reason*."

> It is really weird that I can feel profound beyond words, and ignorant beyond shame at this same moment. So you see, my fine professor, I am unable to grasp the opportunity to show off my efforts. I hope you have understood -- not that understanding will be permitted to change anything -- I realize what making this choice means; I am willing to suffer the consequences of my choice.

He concluded with, "your buddy." And he was. But he got an "F" that day from me. He answered no questions regarding primitivism in American literature, point of view in a Whitman poem, naturalistic philosophy in a story by Hamlin Garland -- or the simple identification of four black writers we had studied.

"If I could only capture my sentiment..." Dear buddy, that is precisely what all writing is about. And how does one reader grasp sentiment? Through patterns and forms and very carefully chosen phrases. And from doing what novelist Ralph Ellison urged me to tell my students: "Read from the inside out." The tone of John's message is conversational, a bit repetitious, sometimes stilted. He's groping. I do not believe he is trying to con me into artificial sympathy.

He comes close to poetry when he writes, "I feel of another time and of another place... profound beyond words, ignorant beyond shame."

He was sincere. Certainly at that time of racial turmoil on campus and of his leadership in student life, his ability was there, brief glimpses surfacing. Everyone has the ability to capture sentiments. Ability stems from intelligence and all mankind is equal in God's sight, created in God's image, even though humanly many inequities exist. If I really follow my convictions, I cannot treat any one student essentially inferior to another. Motivation, stimulation, inspiration will help bring out the full abilities all have.

And they could, in the process, overcome some laziness, sloppy work habits, and disinterest.

My students learned much about motivation and discipline from Nancy Hopper, whose husband is head of the Mount Union art department. Nancy wanted to write books for young teen-agers. After having some manuscripts rejected by publishers, she began making thorough outlines of the books others had published and which were selling well. This way she found the overall plot and style approach which were successful.

Then she adapted those to the stories she wanted to write -- and sold the first of what was to become a delightful series of books for that age group. She had the self-discipline (that's the best) to master the successful technique.

No "grades" were involved at all -- but publication was what she aimed for.

But even if accomplishment isn't there -- yet -- I know that written expression is a treatment to a human being's potential. And I know that everything a young person writes is a reflection of that person's judgment on life as of that moment. Oh, he'll fool me on occasion -- and he'll fool himself just as often; but underneath one may indeed feel "profound beyond words." It's just that the profundity is never beyond the student's ability. That ability comes not only from the brain, but, more importantly, from the heart.

Heady stuff! In 1971 when my text on writing was published, I received a letter from a professor in Pennsylvania who felt I had gone too far.

In the introductory pages of the text, *Man Expressed*, I used an item from an old issue of *The Saturday Evening Post*. It was a totally unreadable set of "directions" on how to fold a piece of paper to make a paper eagle. Now, this item was on the Post Scripts page, a fun thing in which he had a hundred or so dotted lines criss-crossing the sample piece of paper. The directions then merely said, "Follow the lines and there is your very own Paper Eagle!" The item obviously was intended to be in jest with its total lack of clarity. So I appropriated it to illustrate the way we sometimes say nothing in our writing.

Chapter 1 of *Man Expressed* speaks of writing as always dealing with mankind's aspirations.

I quote a poem by Stephen Crane, one by Matthew Arnold, and then to Alfred Kazin, saying,

> when the skies are hanged and oceans drowned
> the single secret will still be man...

I concluded my overview comment then by saying that all writing is "to some degree about the human heart, soul, spirit, that human essence whatever you choose to call it."

In the mail, from the Pennsylvania professor, I received a delightful paper eagle, all neatly folded. The prof had gotten a complimentary copy of the book from the publisher, apparently had read at least the preface and was prompted to show me that he could make the paper eagle from his own directions. Then I saw the writing inside the eagle. He had written this message: "The eagle was fun, but how in hell do you get all that crap about the heart and soul?"

How?

Without our feelings there would be little necessity to write. The symbols would be minimal, shades of meaning would disappear -- and college English profs would readily accept simplistic vocabulary and rote phrasing. Everything beyond "yes" and "ouch" and "no" and "ugh" stems from our inner feelings.

All of this teaching of writing: people ask, do you try to get students to feel just the way you do? To agree with you? No. It's not my job to tell them how to think politically, socially, biologically, financially, morally. I don't have to teach agreements.

But, doggonit, it is my job to teach them how to write well enough that we can know what our disagreements are! When all of us write, express, the feelings of heart and soul so that others comprehend them -- well, the means of solving the disagreements will take care of themselves.

We are all expressions, expressions of what we sense, feel, believe. What more natural activity than to express what we are? The act of getting those thoughts on paper, having them in tangible expression brings its rewards. Writing is therapeutic. B. F. Maiz, concurring, said that all poetry brings elements of mystery and magic to the life of the writer.

Perhaps that is what Margie Moore had in mind two decades ago when she wrote in her journal for my class, "Sometimes I get so tired of writing in this journal! Sometimes I think it's better just to live and forget about interpreting and analyzing life -- but then why do I always turn again to writing, enjoying it?"

8

Who Really Reads?

Out for a leisurely walk across autumn fields, he came upon two white-tailed deer eating corn stubble. He stared at them, they at him in return. An awesomely authentic moment when "the sky seemed to listen with its own ears of light." Man, deer, sky.

And when he told others about the moment, they all asked, "Did you have a camera?"

True, great sharing comes as audiences witness in unison the little dramas, the marvelous color slides, captured moments that may spur conversation, admiration. But silent, one-to-one moments; can they truly be equalled on film?

The person reading is one-to-one with the author in silent, individual pursuit of the experience of a moment of a poem, scene, story.

Paul Williams was glad he didn't have to fiddle around with a light meter, lens, and focus when he spotted the two silent deer. He told of the casual, unhurried sharing. I think I understood.

Many times I was very glad I didn't have to fiddle with a classroom exploration of some hidden meaning, some brownboard list, or "good" questions. Not always looking for a profound question I can ask in a test, something to put them on the spot. Anyway, such an approach makes lousy tests; get enough of them and the students no longer read for insight -- or even pleasure. They start underlining the text for picky details.

On a faculty evaluation sheet a decade ago, a student wrote "Crist revels in picky questions." I've tried to overcome that weakness.

What is "picky" to some, of course, may be delightfully meaningful to another. For instance, in reading a new biography of Walt Whitman -- a man whose poetry I admire and love to teach -- I found out why Whitman may well be special for me: he loved eating buckwheat pancakes. So do I. I'd never raise the observation for text purposes, understand -- but in my lectures I probably alluded to his breakfast menu favorite. I'm just human enough to have done that.

Quiet, reflective reading comes when one simply wants to be absorbed in the book the story, or article. It's a communal experience, author and reader at one.

It's the authentic. The moment when the reader figuratively nods the head, murmurs "I know! I know what you mean!"

The moment in Willa Cather's *My Antonia* when the old immigrant pioneer is to be buried on a knoll on the farm property in Nebraska. The younger generation insists a new highway is coming down that way, would go right over the grave; his widow, however, insisted that was the old man's choice spot, the one he chose, long before roads and cars, to place the roots of his family -- and to be buried.

The chapter ends with Cather saying, "And in later years many who rode down the highway would ask, 'Why does the road bend here? Why does it curve and then continue straight?'"

And I have known such country roads, wondered as well. Out of fiction comes the soft, quiet, reflective moments, authentics which carries wisdom and awareness.

There's an irony at work with reading these days. In a time when we're all caught up in a multitude of liberation movements, we drift away from one of the greatest freedoms we have -- that of individual reading of the entire range of literature. It's easier to have someone else do it for us, stage the 30-second TV news clips, summarize books with 500-word reviews in the papers, and be amused with endless superficial soaps. But imagine: alone with a book, the reader is fully "liberated," on par with the author, uncorrupted by any interference.

Encounters with early American writers can become fringe benefits for those who take the time. In the Mount Union classroom an assignment to read the poetry of Anne Bradstreet from 1676 perhaps seemed a chore. The poems were so remote, so unrelated to the present.

But they only seemed that way. And sometime perhaps Gloria Steinham and Jane Fonda and the others who speak out so strongly about women's liberation will come to see the value of old American literature assignments. I'm in favor of liberating the mind, living up to our potentials. And that's why we can find remarkable insight and valuable information reading, for example, Anne Bradstreet today.

She was, after all, the first true poet of this continent, the "new world." Diverse in topics, skilled in techniques, she offers today a delightful and meaningful cross-section of literature. She was probably the very first to speak out regarding the way women have been "put down" by some of the male population. Read her poem *The Author to Her Book* sometime. In it she says it all -- in two lines in particular:

> If what I do prove well, it won't advance;
> They'll say it was stolen, or else just by chance.

"They," of course, refers to the men of that time. If her poems find acceptance, if the poems pass the test of talent -- "they" will not believe a woman could do so. It's just sheer luck... or sheer thievery.

Liberation comes in many forms. And the academic has its rewards. The textbook provides much of it!

Edward R. Murrow described the daily newspaper as "The world at your doorstep." The definition applies to almost all forms of reading material -- and I think the prof who teaches literature must have the best fringe benefit program going in all organized labor. Digging into reading, one discovers techniques of communication and the lessons from a universe of experience. I like what Mark Harris, who taught then at the University of Pittsburgh, said: "The teacher of literature teaching passionately may often be a far better teacher of writing than the professional writer."

The teacher, too, reads "from the inside out." There probably is no need for any other textbook on writing than a series of solid readings.

Somerset Maugham said, "There is more merit in having read a thousand books than in having plowed a thousand fields." One needs to consider that in light of one's own occupation and needs -- yet surely there is significant commentary here. We need plowed fields, but beyond plowing, beyond grain and fruitage there is another kind of harvest -- that of our own thought, building and pyramiding from the expanse of our reading.

TV's *60 Minutes* did a program on people buying needless life insurance, dozens of policies, primarily because they took the word of glib salesmen, never bothering to read the policies. Many of them,

I fear, simply could not read and the others -- and this is worse -- did not exercise the talents they had acquired.

Paul Chapman, at the time chairman of our department, once posted on his office door the provocative statement: "Those who do not read are no better off than those who cannot read." Mark Twain said it.

How many students miss out on fully understanding the diversity of human experience by confining their spare time to avoidance of reading?

One of the most difficult short stories to grasp at first reading is Faulkner's *Wash*. Yet everything in the story is there in the opening statement. Wash Jones, poor white trash, will do anything to curry the favor of Colonel Sutpen. The time is post-Civil War. The setting is Mississippi. The Colonel has lost his son in the war. Aging, despondent, he must have an heir to carry on the plantation the next generation. In the opening scene, Sutpen is standing beside a creaky bed in Wash Jones' shanty; a young girl -- Jones' 15-year-old daughter -- lies there. Jones stands aside, a newborn baby makes noises -- and the Colonel says, "If you was a mare I'd put you up in the stables."

Therein is the entire tragic story. The reader does not grasp all of this as the scene unfolds; it takes many other pages, some of the background, some of ongoing action, to bring the reader to realize that Jones, doing anything to get in the Colonel's favor, has given him the daughter. And the daughter now has given birth to child, Sutpen's child. It is a girl. And there still is no son to carry the Sutpen name.

If the girl were a horse, Sutpen would at least provide her with a place to stay, something under his roof, his authority. But not this. The child is a girl. Sutpen will do nothing, absolutely nothing.

But the reader *lives* the scene -- and must continue to have it unfold, to fully grasp the significance. That is how literature functions -- no mechanical explanations. Does life offer little push-cards which give answers to all our encounters? What happens is that the reader becomes more and more alert to clues; in turn, good readers should be more aware of meanings of everything around them. The flashing-light scoreboard attracts arena attention, but it seldom appears elsewhere. It's inside our minds where the lights should he burning. And reading helps provide that circumstance.

It is, I note once again, "reading from the inside out."

In a society which has few strictures on what is printed, or distributed, our opportunity is to understand how it is said. We catch techniques and as we read we can ponder the effects of them. Reading, like writing, is an afterthought; it's not ended until we have thought about what we've read. A reflective thought, bending back on the topic and the way it was given to us, enriches.

Of course, sometimes writers may not have material organized for us; they make references which are simply impossible for us to get inside. Like this:

> Dear Editor:
> All I have to say about the Wolf Run Road situation is that I disagree with what Councilman Jones keeps saying. If he's so sure he's right, then why not spend his own money? After all, some of us don't even live there.

We might reach some foggy notion from this that the writer disagrees with somebody named Jones, but beyond all that there is only darkness. Unfortunately, many readers are motivated to send along letters to editors, so sure they (the writers) know what they're saying that they fail to clarify. Professional communicators, however, always draw readers into the writing, leading them to awareness. The difference between reading fiction and reading a recipe, for instance, is that a good writer wants the reader to live, to experience the fiction; the recipe writer wants the reader to follow instructions. In the second we *receive* information; in the former, we *perceive* it. Depending on the mode, our opportunity is always to be equivalent readers -- on a level equal with that of the writer, understanding the techniques and the message. From there it's a matter of lively vocabulary.

Someone may think he has an equivalent reader when he writes, "It was not a very happy party." But equivalency is difficult here; the blandness doesn't stir many emotions. Erma Bombeck, however, can make the statement come alive ; she once wrote, "It was as joyous as George McGovern's victory celebration."

That bad! Now, that's communication. And something to be read. We have life and people and something specific to hold onto. And now the prof is right in the classroom -- teaching basic composition, teaching American literature; it's all the same. Something real to work with.

Jacqueline Jackson, writer of many novels for teen-agers, knows how to encourage writing -- and I'm the beneficiary through reading her works. In one she tells of her four young daughters keeping journals full of questions, curiosities, insights. In a delightful chapter title "Nobody Has No Miseries" their own illustrations show why some writing is good reading above the bland and routine.

"Misery is when you have warts on your hand and nobody wants to hold them when we play ring around the rosie.

"Misery is when you're out camping and you have to go to the bathroom and there are fifty million mosquitoes.

"Misery is when you put a dime in the pop machine and the pop comes out but the cup doesn't and then when the pop is all out, down comes the cup."

Or my favorite: "Misery is when you're following the big old woman around the department store for 45 minutes and then you find out she ain't your mom!"

These are specifics. Picture words which communicate. For now I know what misery is to the girls -- not merely, like, when things don't go good, you know what I mean?

Oren Arnold published more than thirty novels, both for juvenile and adult readers. During the course of a four-hour discussion in 1967 he shared many insights. All were helpful, but none as revealing as the one which developed as I prepared to leave.

"Well, Mr. Crist, you'll be in my next book!"

I was delighted. "Really?"

"Well, not as you, the whole person. I'm not planning on writing your life story! But some facet of your personality. The way you speak or sit, the way you dress. Something will stick in my mind and I'll draw upon it."

So, no biography of the olde prof -- but something real. Writers do not create literature from nothing, nor from pure imagination. No writer begins in a vacuum. In *Poorhouse Fair* John Updike has a character whose chief personality trait is an awkward pronunciation. Another puts toothpicks in his ear, leaving scabrous skin showing.

I remember those authentics. They're in our reading because they're in our lives. Real moments. The time you realized someone was lying to you; the moment you know you're going to lose the basketball game. Such sharp, specific awarenesses are genuine. Literature is built upon genuineness of emotion. Sometimes the writer elaborates on such moments, adding symbols. It occurs, for instance, in a reading of *The Great Gatsby* by Fitzgerald.

In a key scene, Jay Gatsby is standing by the mantel just as Daisy Buchanan enters the room. Gatsby has loved Daisy, has left her for a span of years; now wealthy and famous, he seeks to renew ties with her. In the meantime she has married, yet they are deeply drawn to each other and in this scene Gatsby, nervous, tense, is to have his first look at Daisy after so many years. Can they pick up, so to speak, where they left off years ago? Has time altered things too much?

She enters. Gatsby, awed, then struggling for composure, moves his arm along the mantel to begin striding to her. However, as he does, he accidentally touches the clock on the mantel, causing it to fall to the floor. He pauses, apologizes, tries to return it to its place.

It's an authentic moment for both characters -- and for the reader; certainly for the writer who has, by such contriving, put into focus the issue of time, the time which these two have sought to turn back in their lives. Time, symbolized by a falling clock which is awkward and bumbling -- and which suggests (to the discerning reader) that time will work against Daisy and Gatsby.

Reading from the inside out.

The reader on par with the writer, two as one; a literary communion. The techniques and the experiences are there.

But I know not all of those techniques. Glendon Swarthout was on my list of authors to query when I was on that sabbatical in 1967. As part of my experience, the olde prof wanted to know more and more about how the professional writers accomplished their best; then the prof would share all the techniques with his students in creative writing.

Swarthout achieved fame many years ago for the bestseller about Ft. Lauderdale at spring break -- something I needed to know about! With many of my students following the trail to Florida, a place made popular in the early 1960s by Swarthout's *Where the Boys Are*, it seemed natural for me to interview Swarthout. He had just completed a new home near Phoenix. There on a sabbatical (to do some writing of my own) I located the house, drank in all the costly beauty of it, the obvious results of his literary output. Then I went to a nearby phone to call, identify myself, make an appointment to talk with him. to talk with him.

"Who do you say you are?"

"Prof. Lyle Crist. I teach creative writing back in Ohio." Ohio is somewhat north of Florida.

"Who?"

I repeated, "It's a great opportunity to talk with you about your writing techniques. That way I can take back to Mount Union College --"

"Mount what?"

"To take back your thoughts about good writing, to share them with my students."

"Look, it's taken me all my life to find out what those techniques are --"

"Yes, I know. Well, if I could just have a few minutes of your time --"

"I'm not about to give time to you to blab to everybody else. Then they'll be out in direct competition."

Swarthout did not snarl; he was quite composed. So much so, in fact, that it was evident I had no chance to secure an appointment. And he had a very good point, one I could understand from his perspective.

He was working on a novel later published under the title *The Cadillac Cowboys*. Popular. Breezy. It fetched a good return, I presume.

Back at the brownboard a month later, I told my creative writing class "Commercial writing is a field full of competition. It may not appeal to every one of you."

In all forms of art there are cherished techniques, waiting to be appreciated. Emerson (I keep coming back to him) pointed to the hierarchy which does exist among us, the writers and non-writers: "All books that get fully into the vital areas of the world are written by the affirming and advancing class... who utter what tens of thousands feel, though they cannot say."

That's a profound statement, with deep implications. The trouble is that many students are not quite ready for philosophical ramblings about the necessity for excellent writing and reading. The lure of a romanticized career in literature appeals, especially to those in my creative writing classes. When it comes down to a truly solid piece of writing, something which will take care of the reader's insatiable desire for action (goaded on by endless television programs where thought is unnecessary), right down to the built-in laugh track to remind everybody that what was said was something funny -- even if it wasn't -- well, we can't all achieve it.

I always referred to what has been described by Vincent Starret as one of the "briefest and best short stories in the world." It's a murder mystery written by a little boy in a novel by E.F.Benson. According to Starret, all it lacks is a number of red herrings -- those glamorous sometimes symbolic flourishes which deepen the mystery, adding dimension. "Any reader can put those in for himself," reminds Starret. Here is the complete short story:

Chapter 1
There was once a murderer with yellow eyes and his wife said to him, 'If you murder me you will be hung. And he was hung on Tuesday next.

Finis.

Should the prof teach the depth of Faulkner and Emerson or the downright practical no-nonsense of the little boy?
Both, I say.

9

Encounters of the Campus Kind

He came regularly to the professional writing conferences. They meant much to that elderly gentleman who would not settle for a back seat; he was eager, wide-eyed, with determined appearance. I'd spoken at this particular conference several times through the years; now I shared the platform with three others who, in turn, had discussed poetry, novel writing, non-fiction, and creativity. Such writers' conferences bring a variety both of presenters and listeners.

I knew his type. But I did not mind. He never really bothered me as I wove my way through the assigned topic -- something like "Imagism in Poetry Writing" for the 10:15-11:15 session in Building K of the University sponsoring the conference. Maybe 40 persons, mostly housewives, but a range from high schoolers to retirees in the audience.

He'd be there. If not this particular one, then another who carried the same credentials.

On this particular end-of-the-day session, we four panelists had all conferees -- perhaps 200 -- seated in front of us. It was question period.

"Prof. Crist -- you mentioned this morning Rukeyser's poem about the boy with the haircut; is that in a specific anthology?"

And so they would go. Simple questions. Good exchanging.

I knew this man would ask many. And he did. He had asked in my morning session, had asked in the other sessions -- we panelists referred to it during lunch -- and now he was asking again.

"If I am writing a short story," he began. "Do I block out the whole story first, or go ahead and write the first scene that comes to my mind?"

Someone commented.

He asked again. "If I am writing a poem, do I work for a certain scheme, a certain stanza arrangement or do I just let the words come out regardless of form?"

I shared a personal experience about this.

Someone else asked a question, then the man was at it again. "If I'm stuck in the middle of my novel, should I put it aside for a few days? Or is it better to keep on writing as best I can?"

The celebrity writer to my side stood up; his words avalanched, almost uncontrolled. "Your questions are silly ones," he charged. "You don't really have any questions. You don't even write. You come here and ask questions all day long. You're not a writer. The questions you ask show that. Why come and waste my time and that of the others? You're a dreamer, that's all. And I don't see any need to take time to answer you."

I did not like that, no matter how true it was. I forced a smile and quickly asked for other questions and somehow we concluded the session. But it was awkward.

I've seen that man at every area writing conference. No, he does not write. But he loves to come. I've seen him in different clothing -- and different bodies -- but he is the one who dreams of writing. Perhaps he has dreamed that dream throughout his lifetime. And he will not become a writer in the time remaining.

But we are all dreamers. And if a sense of identity through a writers conference helps that man, should we not allow him to ask his endless questions? He will never discipline himself to try to write. But he enjoys himself.

He may spoil the sessions for others. His questions, seldom profound, waste time for serious writers. I suspect the conference planners have very mixed feelings about his presence -- appreciating the enrollment, worrying over the treadmill effect he creates.

His kind is there, I'm sure, at every writing conference across the nation.

And there are so many others who *do* want to write, to get published.

Getting published can mean so very much. Through my years at Mount Union, however, I've come to learn that some "publishers" have questionable tactics.

It was 1969 when I first encountered one vanity publisher, with a New York address. A writer in another city called me regarding a small book a friend of hers had had accepted by this publisher. She wanted me to go over the contract with her. That contract, though it noted the author would receive "100 free copies" of the book, never stated how many copies would be printed. And the rave letter of acceptance did not seem appropriate as I read the manuscript.

And the price of publication -- to be paid for entirely by the author -- was far beyond what any local printer would bid.

Most disturbing, however, is the fact that over the next 18 years I have seen identical letters of acceptance -- raves -- with but the exception of one paragraph of specific reference to the manuscript.

In 1980 I sent in a test manuscript -- a ridiculous thing titled *Lonely Poems* -- 32 of them composed in a half-hour's time in the office with several students observing. Classic poetry such as:

> People are lonely
> red and black and white and orange
> and purple
> and even those in Kentucky...

The same "rave" letter of acceptance, the same contract guaranteeing "100 free copies" (remember now, in vanity publishing the author pays *all* expenses).

Later, a 30-page "novel" (that's what I called it) sent to this publisher prompted the same exciting acceptance.

This despite such marvelous phrasings as, " 'How are you?' he asked, his mouth opening and closing with each word."

And so in 1983 a student using the name of Richard Allen and several others in my class tried their hand in it -- for a class project.

One "book" was titled *First Love and Other Poems*. At the same time the group also composed a marvelous collection of poems and titled it *Dirt*. Here's a sample of the stuff they put in the manuscript:

Dirty Feathers

> As I looked at the pigeon
> I thought of religion
> And what I could do
> To get that bird in a zoo
> I never got the answer

> I must have been put on hold
> Or maybe God's out of order
> Now wouldn't that be cold?
> Still the squab squatted there
> No clothes 'cause it was bare
> And its feathers fluttered in the wind
> And I wondered if it had sinned
> I guess I'll never know
> All the things I want to
> Like will it want to snow
> When I really don't want it to?

Heady writing! I would have thought that any publisher would merely mutter "that's for the birds" and return the manuscript as quickly as possible.

But no, the identical form letter with raves. In the one paragraph of that form letter referring to the specific writing we find this: "the poems reflect an enviable ability to find optimism in the darkest situation... wit and wisdom abound..."

Fortunately, our class probings into the role of certain vanity publishers was not in the creative writing classes; such responses would have sent me back to Purdue to find out what x equals!

We did our explorations in the Mass Media class, as part of a study of ethics in both print and electronic journalism.

We could justify our time on that basis!

The class learned, had personal experience to see the challenges in ethics. But we worried about others who would not realize, who would send in their money, on the presumption that their writing was actually terrific.

There are writing conferences beyond those nationally advertised ones, conferences of a more personal nature -- and they bring their own intrigues.

It was nice for them to invite us. Shortly after a little collection of my poems, titled *Runaways*, appeared in 1976 came the invitation. Four of my former students -- now married, all with families of their own -- wanted my wife and I to come to one of their homes for dinner in Youngstown, Ohio -- an hour's drive. "We'll celebrate the new book," Nancy Ward Beeghly said.

Further, they had all read the book. That was quite a reward. Francie Magnuson Kerpsack's home was delightful. After dinner the little group gathered in the living room, they asked me to read a few of the poems. They asked if I'd give the background to some of them.

What an idyllic circumstance! I read a few -- the one about the backyard squirrel (his tail in beautiful curved cadence followed the body pattern as he leaped), the one about the turtle (trying desperately to cross a four-lane highway bordering the Mississippi), the one about an old woman in New Orleans (who looked in windows of antique stores and saw only herself), and the one about the honeymooners at the motel (celebrating... and, by golly, I would, too!).

"We've talked about your poems a lot," they said.

Jean said, "We all have our favorites."

Then Nancy again. "Mr. Crist, there's one poem..."

Now it would come out at last, one they didn't like. Poorly written.

"There's this one..."

I tried to help. "You mean it doesn't reflect all those good instructions I gave you in creative writing class?"

"Well, that's not it."

Francie tried to help. "It's one we don't understand."

"Too deep? Too difficult?"

Then the chorus swept over me. "No, not that. We understand it. But it doesn't fit the pattern. The other poems are fun poems, with insights, sure, but they have a touch of light-heartedness, even the one about the turtle. But there's one poem which just has no lightness at all. It doesn't fit the pattern of all the rest."

Jean asked, "Why did you put that one in with the rest?"

Then they opened their books to *Remembrance*. I did not need to, of course. "Why put that poem, so hopeless, in the collection?"

The quietness dominated then. For a moment or so. Then I started to explain. I looked at those wonderful young people -- my children, in a way -- and tried to explain. "Sometimes, " I said, "a poem is the only way you know to express a sentiment. You'll never share it any other way. When I wrote *Remembrance* it expressed not only sorrow, but a deep-inside torment which, at that time, at the time of the writing many years ago, I could not vent any other way. It would have been cheap to do it any other way."

The prof presiding in class again. Probably the smallest of my classes, and yet, in that moment, one of the most important I'd ever have, for I was not talking about a text-book, about wisdom from a great writer, about something for an assignment or a grade or graduation or faculty discussion or dorm pillowtalk. How many times had I spoken of authentics in poetry? Now it was the most important consideration of them all.

"I wrote *Remembrance* because, yes, I did want somebody else to know how I felt; a tangled, confused, emotional feeling of anger that Richard should lose his life in war, high among the clouds in an airplane. And yet with that anger, the epitome of my own frustration, I even sensed the death that I had to fear for my entire lifetime, a physical handicap which made it impossible for me to fly in World War II, to be where Richard was. Which death was worse in such awareness? Death in flight, in the grand adventure which my young mind sought and which would be denied me? Or death -- in a symbolic sense -- by the deprivation which denied even the chance to fly?"

There was no hope in the poem. It did not fit the pattern of the others in the book. "But it was placed there many, many years after it was written so that perhaps someone else would recognize the feeling." Then, perhaps back in the classroom at that moment, I added, "So that you might understand that poetry can cover such a wide range of thought. That is why poetry means so much to me and to all who write it."

The lecture ended. No notes had been taken, no textbooks then closed, no bell to ring. We all came to a communal point. Then we went on to the other poems. The one about the backyard bird (bathing, its measure my pleasure), and the electric mixer (the beater in the batter making clatter but what is better for the eater than the clutter of the butter in the beater?), and the one about dogs (the great Danes in VWs, the poodles in Cadillacs).

She came into the office on schedule; I'd set up the appointment. We needed to have a conference about her short story. It was a good one, but I wanted to suggest some aspects for discussion. If she appeared nervous, it didn't show. This time, I was the one on edge.

After the routine greetings, I asked, "Did you enjoy writing the story?"

She said she'd had some difficulty -- but that, overall, it was a rewarding assignment.

"I think it's very good."

"Really?"

"Definitely publishable. It has all the right ingredients."

She smiled.

"Good characters. Conflict. Resolution. Dialogue reads very well."

She kept on smiling.

"Do you think it's publishable?" I had paused before asking that question.

She had no immediate response, then said, "Well, I don't know. I guess you'd know more about that than I do."

"Editors I know would look with favor on it. Did you plan all along to end it this way -- or would you change anything now that it's been turned in?"

"Well, if you like it, I guess it'll stay. I did think quite a bit about the ending."

"--but you chose this one."

"Yes."

"Why?"

"Well, because, well, it just seemed to be the best way."

"Will you try to publish the story?"

"Not really. I mean, I'm just a student--"

" Don't you think it's any good?"

"Well, I'm glad you like it."

"What grade should I give it?"

"If it's good, well, I'd like a good grade."

"But you don't really know if it's good enough to be published?"

"Not really."

"I think it is."

I spoke slowly that time. Very slowly. She looked at me, then looked down. She seemed preoccupied with her fingers.

I said, "I think it's very publishable." I watched, but her expression did not change. "So much so, in fact, that it has already been published."

I reached under a stack of papers on the desk, fished out the magazine. "You didn't even change the title."

I thought the tears would come.

"Every word. You didn't change one word."

Then she said -- not looking at me -- "I knew that's why you wanted me to come in this afternoon."

I said she'd done a fine acting job up to that point.

Then the tears came. "I didn't think I could write a story good enough. I wanted a good grade."

To her credit, she did not ask for a second chance. She accepted the "F" with some dignity. A senior, this placed her graduation in jeopardy; it was spring term. "It goes as an 'F.' Your other papers have had good grades -- perhaps the average will still allow a passing grade for the course. We'll watch the rest very closely." I arranged a conference with the Dean.

As she teaches today -- and does a fine job -- perhaps she recalls, too, that incident. I'm confident she treats carefully her own students who feel inadequate for some assignments.

The pageant of years brought endless moments of awareness that the grade is, for so many, the ultimate judgment. A letter that came a few weeks after the end of the fall semester in the late 1970s brought it home again.

The envelope had the colorful figures of an Easter basket; golds and greens and reds. The stationery inside matched. Pleasant, jolly motif. But the message read otherwise.

"...When I saw that ugly, awful minus sign after my grade of 'B' on the Registrar's notice, I cringed. I thought I earned a 'B.' I thought you said it looked like I'd be getting a 'B' in creative writing. And then I saw that awful, hideous minus sign after the 'B.' It is disgusting..."

The letter ended, "Is that all that you really thought of my work? That awful minus sign?"

I answered the phone, something about a schedule change for Margaret; yes, it would be all right with me. Then Phil came in with a question about Washington Irving; did he get all his ideas from his travels to Europe? Then Sue popped in; "Behaving yourself old man?" Now, how could she think otherwise?

Then Jim Walton, my colleague, waved in the corridor. "Meeting at three. Don't be late, friend!"

Couldn't be. I was late the last time and missed the entire discussion on the proposed dropping of the foreign language requirement in our department.

The letter was still in my hand. I checked my grade book; she had earned a "B-." And that isn't a bad grade at all -- not if "C" is to be the average. So "B-" was above that; from my secluded, professorial view, it was a good grade. Remembering the student's short story and set of poems at term's end -- I didn't give final exams in creative writing -- I had no doubt about the rightness of the grade. It was nearly 2:45 now. Three classes done for the day. Time to walk to the administration building, check with the Dean about the honors convocation coming up, still make the meeting.

Looking somewhat grim, I went down the hall; no elevator this time. I needed to sort out things. Three flights down, then through the lobby, busts of Orville Nelson Hartshorn and Ira 0. Chapman on display -- the first founded the college, the second for whom the building was named a century ago. Did Hartshorn ever have letters from students?

Down the long, straight walk, nods to two or three who came the other way. Across the street, into the building, ask about the Dean. He's out till four. All right. I'll catch him later. Maybe that department meeting will be over by then.

Down to the Registrar's office. "Hello Mr.Crist!" They're quite pleasant there. "What can we do for you this time?"

Sometimes it's a look at an application blank, sometimes an advance schedule, sometimes the college calendar -- especially if I've misplaced my catalog once again; it happens at least weekly.

"Need a change of grade form."

"Going to downgrade somebody?"

I took my pen, wrote the student's name, signed mine, then noted "Present grade: 'B-.' " "Grade to be changed to --"

I wrote in "B."

The secretary was still smiling. "Right? Going to down-grade somebody?" Perhaps my stare was unnerving. It was a bit of time before I responded to the inquiry.

"Yes. I think that's a good word for it."

I walked back to Chapman Hall in time for the meeting.

I thought about something John Fisher had written.

Former editor of *Harper's*, he put down some light-hearted thoughts on a mythical university -- old "curmudgeon U" as he dubbed it. At this school there would be no dormitories -- students would live wherever they could find places. The faculty would have no tenure -- they would be paid by merit and be dismissed when they botched their jobs. Further, would write summations of the students' overall achievements in class. Tests? They'd be given whenever the students requested them -- and students would come to realize the value of such tests. Students could enter or leave any class or course whenever they chose -- but they would have to deposit $1 in the till each time they entered a classroom; professors got a percentage of the take and thus the better ones would make the most money. All students may receive loans to ensure their full schooling regardless of family or financial circumstance -- but the loans must be paid back at a one percent interest each year for the rest of their lives. This would make fund-raising automatic for the college, relieving the President for more important matters.

On occasion, old profs think about such frivolities with just a touch of serious mein.

Or is studying to be a second-hand aspect of the college experience? My entire outlook on what I thought was a fairly agreed-to approach to education by college personnel came undone in 1982. I had read a story in *The New York Times* News Service that an Associate Dean at Tufts University in Massachusetts was disturbed about the matter of priorities on that campus.

According to the news story, "We've had fewer parties than in the past in freshmen dorms; there are more complaints from freshmen about noise at night and there have been some requests to keep the library open 24 hours a day. It's sad. The kids, especially the freshmen, are succumbing to the pressure of the economy and to their parents' anxieties over the rising cost of education..."

I wrote the Dean, noting that "As a long-time English professor, I'd think that such trends are causes for rejoicing. Or am I completely out of it? Or is Tufts a place where partying and loud noise are the primary activities? Or is the quote distorted in the article? I'd like to know... I'd appreciate a little bit of dialogue with you."

Never had a reply. I wrote again some three months later. Never had an acknowledgement of any kind.

It's sad, isn't it? Kids succumbing to parents' anxieties, kids wanting to use the library more often, kids trying to keep the dormitory noise down.

Really sad.

Professional meeting time -- in summer, no time from classroom duties deprived. Washington, D.C. in July, the cherry blossoms gone, but bright, active faces of delegates and general membership. My initial encounter with this professional speakers organization.

"Did you know about the poetry section? It meets tomorrow morning. You'd enjoy sharing some of yours -- a general reading at 10:30."

The information was much appreciated; I hadn't brought along any of my poems, but I could recall them readily. That evening I took some of the hotel stationery, jotted down two poems -- a vignette about architecture and an insight with rhyme regarding teaching. Yes, they'd do; the kind I was proud of.

At 10:15 I showed my badge to a woman at a table near the door. "Do I sign up here for the reading?"

She was efficient. "Just let me see it." Her arm shot up, fingers took the stationery. My poems were in longhand.

"I hadn't known about the reading before coming," I explained. "But I jotted them down last night."

Her eyes rocketed up the pages, then shot downward across their expanse. "All right. You can read these." It seemed a bit odd -- she had done no real reading of them. So quick.

Inside, I found about a hundred others. In front, a woman talking about "my world of poetry." Then the readings began, each name, as it was called by the chairwoman, the object of some plaudit. "Next is Mr. Smith, such a good friend of mine. His themes are about life itself, and I so enjoyed reading them last night."

I must have missed a pre-reading session. Anyway I listened. Smith and then Jones and then others. Maybe five or six. Two poems each, with the usual song of praise about the "lovely poems" to be read.

Then came Mr. Johnson (or Brown or whatever). Again the "nice man, nice poems" statement. Mr. Johnson's poems were, I had to admit, better than the others. Applause for him was not just perfunctory. "Well," he said, acknowledging the very positive response," since you liked those, I'd like to read a new poem -- one which I just composed this morning. I think you'll like it, too--"

He held the paper in front of him, cleared his throat, and then the chairwoman spoke. "Did I see this poem?"

"No, I just wrote it this morning."

"Then I haven't read it?"

"No. But I think you'll like it."

"I need to see the poem."

"Well, it's just a short one --"

"Let me see the poem, Mr. Johnson." Sternly now. She spat out the words.

"Well--"

"The poem. Before you read it."

Mr. Johnson handed over the piece of paper to her. I looked around the room; quietness engulfed, but no one said anything, not even a whisper. Obviously, the chairwoman had chaired this session for years -- and years; she was in charge.

I do not know if she approved of his morning poem. I had gotten up and left by then. Never before did a hotel lobby atmosphere seem so clean to me.

Although I was appalled at what had taken place, at least I knew I had gained a bit of wisdom. I knew then what the woman at the table was looking for -- why it only took her a few seconds to give approval.

And this -- a *professional* meeting.

Novelist Ellen Glasgow is reported to have said that all she ever wanted was adulation. Her honesty is infectious. I admit to the same aspiration when it comes to writing; a little praise goes a long way. Yet I heard someone at a conference on the teaching of writing say that teachers give too much time to praising little kids about their finger painting -- and the same with college students. The speaker said that mud on the streets is good, but merely to smear mud around is bad. Yet we go bananas praising little kids who have done nothing more on construction paper but smear around a little colored mud.

How much praise, how much adulation should the prof have for students? Part of the answer is in the prof's own desires for himself. I'll take adulation readily, even though it's never come to me in excess with regard to my own writing skills. Probably the finest tribute I've received came from the teacher in a grade school in Texas. Somehow she had gotten a copy of a collection of my poems -- and shared an observation with me. The poem is strictly a fun poem, prompted by the awareness that among the 650,000 words were enough to capture both the sound as well as the sentiment which was mine when I knew our old electric mixer was at work in the kitchen:

>I like the clatter
>of the batter
>in the beater
>though it's neater
>if the latter
>doesn't splatter
>yet the pounding
>of its sounding--
>though it's frightful--
>is delightful
>for the clutter
>of the butter
>in the beater

is much better
than the clitter
of a fritter
getting fatter
in its batter
when the matter
in the beater
finds my platter.

Who can utter
words to flatter
better than a beater?

What is sweeter
for the eater
but the chatter
of the batter
in the beater?

    Alas, some people think of poetry as a commodity to be carefully stored on shelves, taken down only when it's Christmas or when someone dies. Obviously the electric mixer -- if, indeed, it is a poem -- has not one shred of serious vein to it. But it does have its place.

    And the letter from Texas delighted me above any academic praise I might have received (which, in fact, never came -- but that's beside the point!). This grade school principal wrote to tell me that *Beater* was being used by all the fourth graders in her school -- as accompaniment to their rope-skipping during recess period. "It may become a habit around here!"

    That, I submit, is something to make the olde prof's heart feel good. With that I can try (almost successfully) to ignore the "praise" of one reviewer of the earlier writing text of mine, *Man Expressed,* who noted, "The cover of the book certainly is exciting."

    I didn't think I'd surpass more than the word of my Texas correspondent; but in the late 1970s, when two senior music majors on campus set *Beater* to music, and I heard it played and sung by them during a recital, I fully realized that all that I'd ever taught about poetry was true.

    We build. Everything pyramids, nothing is alone. *Beater* became important when children skipped rope to its tempo -- and had fun doing so; it became meaningful when I realized that the rhythm in my own mind in that silly little exercise had a response in the minds of others, exemplified by the music.

You never stop learning.

10
Thinking

I'm not aware of anyone whose life has been made better, who has achieved great things merely because he had money for tuition, plopped into a lecture hall seat, and flipped quickly through some textbooks. You and I are born equals, products of some creative force (called by various names, and sometimes we argue over the names when we mean essentially the same quality) that includes us in its expression. Who said that English 205 ever determined the worth of one individual over another?

A literature class may, however, have something to do with the quality of our thinking.

To read intelligently doesn't mean to read into something that which isn't there; it does mean to read with full awareness of what is going on. Someone has created a sequence; the reader should be as deeply involved in deciphering what is said as the person concocting the sequence. This can be carried to extremes, of course; I must confess I've never gotten through *Finnegan's Wake* by James Joyce. And Joyce must confess that he once said that the demand he placed upon is readers was that they spend the rest of their lives reading and studying his works.

That's a bit much. I'd rather go for a ride on my moped or watch the squirrels in my back yard. Or cut the grass. Or read Dr. Seuss. Or teach a class in creative writing.

But we all need to be on par with authors -- because without that equivalency, we can all be fooled. Miserably. Back in the 1960s I showed a lit class the account of the heroic efforts of one Ning Hseuh-chin as reported in the *Peking Review*. Ning Hseuh-chin was a Communist fighter of the seventh company of the P.L.A. unit under the Lanchow command in China when Mao Tse-Tung was at his height. On duty in the Peking railroad station, Ning Hseuh-chin observed a group of Red Guard soldiers enter. According to the newspaper account as reprinted in the magazine, they were "educated youths determinedly embarking on the road indicated by Chairman Mao."

At this point, according to the article, Ning Hseuh-chin said to himself, the glowing words in direct quotation: "With these youngsters developing as successors to the revolutionary cause, we can be sure that our Party will never turn revisionist and our state will never change its political colour. We revolutionary fighters should follow Chairman Mao even more closely, fear no hardship or danger, dare to charge forward at any crucial moment, and stand up to all tests. We should stand sentry and fight well in defense of Chairman Mao's revolutionary line."

Well and good, if you like that kind of stuff. At this point, according to the Peking newspaper story, some of the Red Guard soldiers became confused as they crossed the maze of tracks; several were dazzled by lights of a fast train approaching. A tragic accident was imminent. At this crucial moment, Ning Hseuh-chin recalled Chairman Mao's great teaching: "To die for the people is weightier than Mount Tai." Again in glorious direct quotation. With this, he dashed forward (or was it "charge forward at any crucial moment...?) and pushed the soldiers out of the way of the incoming train -- just in time; but Ning Hseuh-chin himself was struck by the train and fatally injured. The rest of the article is a tribute to his bravery.

"Well, what do you think of that article in the *Peking Review*?"

"Real sense of dedication."

"He must really believe his political leaders." Both comments from the first row.

I tried again. "But what of the story itself and its impact upon you? What do you see in this specific phrasing?"

Nothing.

I have much work to do.

To read discerningly! To realize that those long, trumped-up quotations were just that! How in the dickens could anybody know Ning Hseuh-chin's exact thought pattern? The young man is hit directly by a speeding train and carted away! Those long, fully developed sentences, the specific quotes -- who had any way of knowing even the essence of what was going through his mind?

But it made excellent propaganda. On that score I give the *Peking Review* an "A." My students, however, flunked the test. Ning Hseuh-chin didn't roll over on the stretcher and smile at those around him, saying, "Well, fellas, I want you to record exactly what I have been thinking. If I conk out in recovery here is what I had in my mind. Jot this all down now in beautiful direct quotes for posterity -- and the *Peking Review*."

Words are never without thoughts behind them. Put the thoughts together and you have the depth or the shallowness of the concepts. Make judgments. Read newspapers. Don't confine English to esoteric poems or long-gone novels. Read *Silas Marner* if you wish, but don't forget the *Gary Tribune* or the *Dallas News*; they will help sharpen your awareness. For instance, the story of the exhortation in the *Gary Tribune* from the National Steel Company. It was concerned in 1976 about the lack of freedom Americans would have in selecting their automobiles should some federal proposal go into effect regarding the size of cars. According to the news story, an executive wrote each employee, asking all to bombard Washington with protests.

"How would YOU enjoy packing the kids into a subcompact for a vacation trip simply because that's all you could buy? If YOU want to decide what size of car you need and can pay for, write your congressman."

What was behind all the words, of course, was the fact that less steel would be used in smaller cars, so get on the stick. Tell Congress we want more steel used so that our paychecks stay up there.

Little in life is simple. Our stand on any issue had better come from careful thinking. Some years ago when the family had a small country place, the well was not functioning properly. We called the plumber to check it out. On a warm July afternoon we gathered at the well, watched as he checked the depth of the water; he did this by taking a long rope, looping it around a block of wood -- then lowering the block of wood to the water. After many, many yards of rope had been used, he made contact, fished a bit, then hauled up the piece of wood. Looking at it carefully, he exclaimed -- with an air of triumph -- "There's your trouble! See -- only about a half inch of the wood is wet. You've got a dry well!"

Actually, he was close. We had a dry plumber.

A letter-writer in the *Akron Beacon-Journal* two decades ago quoted the *Bible* as an authority for capital punishment. "Remember," he said, "the *Bible* says it plainly -- an eye for an eye."

Powerful reasoning, especially if you don't read the entire chapter and verse. The opposite emerges, but the writer stopped when he found just what he wanted for his own purposes.

And so did I in the National Steel account a short while back. But I want students probing everything in the media, not because the media is warped or wrong, but because our minds are capable of seeing through such shaping when it occurs. And to exercise our minds is one of the reasons we teach English.

The musty minutes of the Nonpareil Club of Mount Union College contain an interesting illustration of what might be called circular reasoning. I haven't quite figured out in what category it goes. In any event, in the minutes, for January, 1889, meeting (no, I wasn't on the faculty then! I read of this in Mount Union's historical files) of this group we find the following entry:

> The motion of Mr. P. that this is strictly a private dance and no one be allowed or admitted without an invite was by permission of the second recalled and stated thus: that we have an invitation dance and admit anyone whom we thought was admittable, which was carried.

I have pondered this for years -- not since 1889, but ever since I came across it in the college library volumes. Certainly does show the depth of phrasing and implication. I think it does.

But, then, what does it say?

To think through! How easily we all are manipulated because we don't think deeply enough. In the Joan Little murder trial in North Carolina in 1975, we found the press plastering photos of Miss Little on her way to court, coming out of court, talking with reporters -- in all instances with a copy of *To Kill a Mockingbird* clutched in her hands. The trial was a classic white-black confrontation with overtones of prejudice and bias built into practically every aspect of the case.

I do not pass judgment on the decision; it was a sordid affair at best and the defendant probably had every right to take the action she did. But I'm intrigued by the deliberate manipulation of emotion and thought by her attorney, one who has garnered high fees. "You must orchestrate the press," said the attorney. He did. *To Kill a Mockingbird*, a novel full of racial implications applicable to the accusations against Joan Little, as part of it.

He added, "The country works that way."

So we are all the audience while the magicians create their illusions, work their magic to amuse us.

And *Time* and *Newsweek* and all the others display pictures of Larry Flynt, of porno magazine fame at his trial with wife always at his side, always holding his hand. And Maureen Dean was always photographed seated behind husband John during the Watergate TV spectacular.

We have all the props on stage to influence the audience.

Teaching English involves clear thinking, the ability to ferret out facts, sort out emotions -- and to help others understand illusions which are created by.

Unfortunately, our lives are molded all too often by slogans and sayings lacking substance. It's the prof's business to motivate students to notice blandness and vagueness in such statements. Again, the daily paper readily becomes the textbook. Here's another letter-to-the-editor, in its entirety:

> On January 1, 1863 slavery was abolished. However, the slave-owner mentality lives on in the minds of our policy makers and power brokers who think of the people only as figures on a piece of paper to be manipulated for the benefit and enrichment of the government, the corporation, and even the men and women entrusted to determine the constructive national policy.

Where are the specifics? Where is the case against the power brokers? Like *what*? Yet, non-thinkers, impressed with the letter, will say "right on!"

The Iranian people were swept into frenzies of emotional outbursts against the United States during the long hostage crisis. There may have been genuine concern and basis for some aspects of the past, but those who waved fists by the hundreds of thousands massed in city streets were all too plainly orchestrated, following lines of emotional generalities and leadings. One Irani student with whom I discussed the situation said, "But what can they do? You can't go against the government. Too dangerous."

Many nations function that way.

And sometimes educational systems. I recall reading an article by Dmitri Simai telling of his experience as a youngster in a Russian school system. He had written a paper on the poetry of Alexander Pushkin, noted Russian writer. His paper received a failing grade. In the margin his teacher had written, "This is nothing more than a series of your own opinions. Who would ever be interested in them?"

For a starter, the student would be interested. But the system then allowed for no such expression: learn the "facts," and repeat them blindly... personal opinion, personal thought -- something to be avoided in education.

Yet it is one of the most precious opportunities we have. Are we taking advantage in the United States of the opportunity to live up to our potential as *thinkers*?

Who is thinking? Norman Cousins found out when he regularly duped readers of his *Saturday Review* -- a magazine not known for a low-IQ readership. Cousins every so often would put in fake letters-to-the-editor -- then watch as the responses from upset "readers" came in. For instance, in one he wrote about a congressman -- A.F. Day -- who had introduced a bill to outlaw golf courses throughout the United States. The irate letter writer, one K. Jason Sitewell, noted that A.F. Day's grandfather had died of apoplexy in a sand trap many years before (33 chip shots and never got out!) and this was a narrow-minded course of revenge.

Few noted the date of the issue -- the Saturday closest to April Fool's Day, 1975 -- hence the name "A.F. Day."

Golf Digest magazine did not catch on! Its strong editorial exhortation for readers to protest to their elected representatives brought an avalanche of letters to Washington. At least until somebody checked out "Congressman" A.F. Day's name.

Several years later Cousins again writing under the name of K. Jason Sitewell noted a pending bill by one Congressman A.F. Day which would establish a national computerized Christmas card register, eliminating all individual Christmas cards because they were the cause of the destruction of too many trees. If the bill passed, all persons would send a list of names to Washington, D.C. by December 1; the national computer would spew printouts to be sent to various households listing "names of all those wishing you a Merry Christmas and a Happy New Year."

Again the date of the Saturday nearest to April Fool's Day was at the bottom of the letter-to-the-editor page. Few were thinking enough to reach the right conclusion. Many Congressmen were bewildered by the hundreds of protest letters.

Again, Cousins printed a review of a new book titled *Illegal Separation*, a book proving that there were 816 illegalities in the Declaration of Independence and thus the "United States" was still part of the British kingdom. The book was published by the "Ayeff Daye Press of Dublin." The giveaway date at the bottom of the page. Nobody had to be a college graduate to catch on. Any thinking person would have spotted all the clues, synthesized them, put the together. Unfortunately, a college degree does not guarantee that the reader will be a thinker; the degree should, but does not. We all have much to learn about that.

A college degree is not the end product; it is, rather, something akin to the experience of reading a poem, line by line. We can pronounce the words, see their sequence, follow the structure, master the meter -- and conclude. We turn the page, complete our task. Chances are, however, that some will read the poem and understand it; others will not grasp its implications. Yet we can say that all who turn the page have become "familiar" with the poem.

Those who understand the poem will find it affecting them, molding them, prodding their thought! It will tease and taunt, making them touch doors they otherwise would walk by; force them to be thinking more deeply about daily encounters, enable them to realize the need to ask more questions.

Lines will pop into their thought; they may share the lines, but in any event the lines will never leave their thought; they will be urging thought to go over the present horizon.

Ever have a poem do that for you?

Robert Frost wrote of the winter heave of earth which, as the cold came and receded, sent stones spilling to either side of the man-made stone fences which separated New England properties. "Something there is that doesn't love a wall," he began, "that sends the frozen ground swell, spilling boulders so that two could pass abreast..." You read the entire poem and you say "That's nice. It's about two guys and a fence." And you walk away to check out the car wash or brush your teeth or watch the Super Bowl.

"Nice. Don't build walls some places."

There are lines other than those of football scrimmage, however.

Seeing the neighbor lug the boulders back into place, Frost speculates a bit more in the poem. Who is responsible for the cracks in the wall? "I could tell him elves, but I'd rather he found out for himself."

Elves? The poet later speaks of his neighbor this way:

> Armed like some stone age savage.
> He walks in darkness, it seems to me...

Now the poem begins to stick. Darkness. Ignorance. Blind, stupid tradition. Ringing lines and references. You perceive that the poem is not a statement about two gentlemen walking alongside a stone fence which separates their properties, picking up stones which have fallen as a result of winter's heave and drop. But you sense something else, a statement about ignorance, blind tradition, about a stone-age thought, not fallen stones.

"Good fences make good neighbors," the neighbor says. And he knows nothing else except that traditional line. When does it make good neighbors? At all times? As we wonder we find ourselves in multiple meanings. Two in one. Frost once said that when you learn to say one thing in terms of another then you are thinking. And my students listen to all this, and some say, "Fine for you, but I can't master all of that. In all my schooling I've learned to think and speak directly. Don't expect me to master this double-meaning stuff in one term, prof!"

And some say, "I just can't be a writer, a good one like the ones you talk about in class all the time. I can't think that way."

And I think of a little book, *I Never Saw Another Butterfly.* I throw away my text on writing (the one written by the "old codger"), go back to the office for this slim volume of poems published by the Jewish Refugee Society. Poems from little kids in Germany and Czechoslovakia in the late 1930s and early 1940s. Kids taken from their homes and families because of their ancestry, their only crime. Little kids, 6, 8, 10, 14. Kids who spent weeks, perhaps months in a concentration camp in Czechoslovakia, an old castle named Terezin, before they were sent to the gas chambers. Kids who had crayons and paper scraps and brief lives, kids who sensed their fate and who wrote poems with simple double meanings without the benefit of any of my college classes at Mount Union, without benefit of sophisticated high school curriculum kids with possibly no school at all.

I've read no poems more creative than this brief statement by a little girl named Franta Bass; the compilers of the book think she was 11 years old when she combined the tragedy of a boy's impending death with the beauty of a flower about to bloom:

> A little garden,
> Fragrant and full of roses.
> The path is narrow
> And a little boy walks along it.
>
> A little boy, a sweet boy,
> Like that growing blossom.
> When the blossom comes to bloom
> The little boy will be no more.

The boy is destined for the gas chambers -- even though he may not know it, Franta Bass does. And she says, "When the blossom comes to bloom..." What a remarkable, awesome coupling of a lovely bud that, in light of the message, we now want to wither, fade, stop its growth because in its blossoming time the little boy will be taken to the gas chambers. Beauty and disaster combining, not "you will die in ten days" but "when the flower comes to bloom..." Saying one thing in terms of another.

A student says, "You expect too much of me, prof."

I say, "I expect you to be a human being. As much a human being as Franta Bass."

And student and prof come closer now.

Others have coupled beauty with death. Gerhard Manly Hopkins wrote of the time of falling leaves, a topic popular with all poets. He spoke of the time of change of inescapable change:

> Margaret, are you grieving
> over goldengrove unleaving?

She grieves and you do and I do, seeing the leaves come down, the trees becoming somber and naked. Hopkins concludes with a devastating, yet meaningful couplet 14 lines later -- bringing the girl and the falling leaves into single focus:

> It is the curse that man was born for--
> it is Margaret that you mourn for.

We subconsciously see ourselves falling. Words carrying double meanings. How do I discuss the fragile and meaningful nature of words? How to convince a class of the double meanings implicit in literature? How to get the class to think about them?

I become reckless. I let my eyes fall on one of the delightful coeds in the class. "You're a beauty," I say. She is unsure; the class picks up interest. The old prof stays his distance -- behind the lecture stand -- but continues to gaze at the young lady. "I think I am falling passionately in love with you." Somebody giggles.

I'll go to those 650,000 words to find some which will explain my passion. Ah! I have it: "When I look at you I am aflame!"

Two fellows clap hands. "Nice job old boy."

"OK?" I ask the girl, who has appreciated the attention of those who have followed this strange business. "Not bad at all," she smiles. "I'll buy it!"

Now the English prof comes to the surface. I tell her, "I can give you the exact sentiment with other words."

"The one about you're aflame? Like what?"

"Like, 'You burn me up!'"

And so the entire intrigue is destroyed, the meaning of individual words altered in sequence. We laugh, have a point.

"What if I said, 'Darling, when I look at your time stands still!... not bad?"

She agrees.

"But what if I had said, you have a face that would stop a clock!'"

We laugh. "If I had said, 'Darling, I'm really bent on seeing you tonight,' you would have been pleased?"

She agrees.

"Same sentiment with other words: 'The sight of you will double me up.'"

And now we are all thinking more clearly about our vocabulary, about the sometimes fragile nature of words.

It's a vocabulary which always changes. Words, like humans, have life-spans. Some may even be aborted. Some lead very long, perhaps we might ever say "dull" lives. But some change.

Brinton Turkle, who grew up just across from the Mount Union campus, was reading the classic *Over the River and Through the Woods* poem, for instance -- and found that words change. A writer and illustrator, Brinton had been asked to do a series of illustrations for a new printing of the poem by Lydia Child. "I'd better read all of it to get the feel of it," he told himself and began. Midway through the poem he came to this couplet:

> Old Rover shakes his pow
> With a loud bow-wow...

Brinton was startled, concluding that the poet has tried to rhyme "paw" with "bow-wow," succeeding miserably. However, he checked the dictionary just to be sure -- and found out that in the 19th century a "pow" was, indeed, a "head." Thus Rover was doing the right thing -- and the poem had a legitimate rhyme. Words can be seen is so many symbolic ways. From the light-hearted to the very meaningful.

I learned a totally different appreciation of words in 1972.

That year I had gone to Chicago, doing research for my biography of Dr. Richard Kinney, blind and deaf president of the Hadley School for the blind and a 1953 graduate of Mount Union. Dick lost his vision when he was seven, lost his hearing when he 21.

Mrs. Elizabeth West called me, having heard I was working on the book: she had something she wanted to show me, which she found was of great interest to Dr. Kinney. "I call it a 'Kinneymobile,'" she said. "It's just a series of things in sequence on a string. Each thing is symbolic of a word."

A Kinneymobile is what I'd call a "touch charade." By touch -- and remembrance -- Dick would perceive words, link them in sensible sequence. Since I've mentioned Robert Frost a few pages back, let's consider a 'Kinneymobile' which represents another one of Frost's best-known poems; it's in all the high school anthologies.

Start with a flat piece of cardboard in octagonal shape. Down the string attach a small piece of wood. Then a tuft of cotton. Conclude with another flat cardboard in crescent shape. Touch the four items (eyes closed, to get the feel of it!) and you get four key words of the poem's title.

It's *Stopping by Woods on a Snowy Evening*.

Sure, the sequence on the string could have suggested "Eight Sides on a Hospitalized Banana" -- but Dick knew no poem by that title. Symbols for words which themselves are symbols for thoughts. We think them through.

Kinneymobiles seemed to me fine teaching tools; they illustrate the symbolic aspect of words, they discipline the relation of thing with thought, and offer good projects for students to develop their own mobiles. I introduced them into my creative writing classes shortly after learning of them.

In fact, I made a requirement that each student in the class must devise at least one good Kinneymobile, then present it to the class. "And we'll have volunteers, those who will close their eyes, touch the mobiles, see if they can figure out the proverb, line from poem, or song title -- all on the basis of touch alone." Years later, I was still requiring Kinneymobiles. In my office the walls were covered with them. One which drew much attention was suspended directly behind my chair -- a novel sight at least. A cheese grater, followed by a tuft of fur, and concluding with a small imitation bee complete with wings and popping eyes.

"My God!" one textbook salesman exclaimed, "what do you use that for?" He was visibly moved himself, having not even gotten to the sales pitch about a new creative writing text written by some fellow at Columbia University.

"It's a Kinneymobile." I enjoyed his confusion. "That one is a title of an American novel of the twenties."

Further explanation brought his deep thought, then, to the solution. Finally he pleaded, "Gimme the author."

That would settle it, of course. "F. Scott Fitzgerald. It's one of his best known."

A long moment -- then the sudden grin and the shout of victory. "I've got it! The Great Gatsby!"

"Grate!" Fur meant "cat" and the "bee" merely finished the word.

Others on walls create their own conversations, but one Kinneymobile which did not make the office walls -- in fact, thrown out because it didn't qualify -- was the simplest of all submitted over the years. The student took a piece of black construction paper, scissored it into a heart shape, and suspended it from the string. Just one reference.

"The author is Joseph Conrad," she said, after the student with closed eyes had pondered the shape for some time without success. But the rest of the class got the answer quickly -- "Heart of Darkness."

The student with closed eyes, however, did not understand -- nor would Dick Kinney have understood.

And you, too, know why this one did not qualify -- for a genuine Kinneymobile, a touch-charade for a deaf and blind person. You do see the problem, don't you?

My favorite of all the Kinneymobiles students have made in creative writing classes is the title of a song which probably played an important role in the students' lives.

A pop can. Then a circle. Then two stamps.

"Pop can... circle... stamps." Say it a few times and you realize that the songs is "Pomp and Circumstance" -- played at their graduation ceremonies in high school.

We're talking about thinking.

Looking back over the intrigues with Kinneymobiles, I can understand even more now why one student more than all others enjoyed the assignment. She was a good writer, conscientious, and perhaps that would be enough explanation why she not only submitted a good mobile -- but continued submitting them over and over. I must have had a dozen excellent ones from her during the six weeks remaining in the term after Kinneymobiles were introduced to the class. She didn't do them for bonus grades, not for glory, not for brownie points in any way. Barbara Fohl, a 1974 graduate, kept making them because they meant something more to her than these did to others in the class.

She was blind.

The symbolic implications of words are of meaning to the students who find other symbols and meanings in their lives. Reading, thinking, experiencing go hand in hand. In his book *The Awakened Eye*, Ross Parmenter tells of learning about meanings via editors who did not care. As an aspiring writer he came to know, editors were not interested in the slant of light, an eyebrow raised, a moment of awareness; the "big story" of action meant more to them. But Parmenter found his own more symbolic experiences.

Dejected by the failure of several manuscripts to sell, he went to the 49th Street pier in New York City on a hot Saturday in August to cool off. Gulls were overhead. He noted that they dipped and rolled in interesting patterns and for the first time he began to ask some questions about "little things" and their meanings: how did gulls brake, for instance, for landings?

He remembered as a boy being taught to bring in a sailboat by veering directly into the wind at the last moment at the pier, the impact upon the spread canvas bringing the boat to a stop. Without pressure of deadline, he watched the gulls, realizing now that they always landed into the wind. The birds knew something of wind and wing, pressure and gravity. Parmenter mused on this simple observation, found his own consciousness raised considerably. A sense of renewal from simple observation.

And back to Chapman Hall, room 109, the prof introduces William Cullen Bryant and the wild ducks to the American Lit class, 9 to 10 a.m. on a chilly January morning, floppy coats and gloves tossed askew across vacant seats. Notebooks out, the text in pouches, tote bags inscribed with college symbols.

"*To a Waterfowl* by Bryant," I intone, "brings us a message of observation and interpretation." American lit exam in mid-March will have a question: "Cite an instance of an author making simple observation, followed by interpretation." Those who have reviewed their notebooks from this day will do satisfactorily on this one.

They may, in fact, do too well.

For if Bryant is the only author I assign and *To a Water Fowl* the only illustration I use they will feed them back to me -- and I will ponder again the tiles on the floor.

At a time of career decision, in the early 1800s, Bryant observed ducks migrating, realized that somehow, those birds know where they should go, what "career" decision they should make. And he wrote, "He who from zone to zone guides thy skyward flight/ surely in the way that I must go, will guide my steps aright..."

Allen Boone tells of a different type of awareness. His book *Kinship With All Life* probes the intelligence of animals. A Hollywood writer of the 1920s, Boone began thinking as he sat at his desk that Strongheart, a movie stunt dog he was caring for, would like to roam the nearby mountainside -- it was a perfect day for such hiking. As Boone contemplated, Strongheart left the room, returning shortly with Boone's hiking boots in his mouth, placed them at Boone's feet. What line of communication here?

After they climbed the mountain, then rested at a viewpoint overlooking the city, Boone became aware that Strongheart was quite still, sitting, head unmoving. At what was the dog staring? Roads below? The cars? The smoke from factories? Animals in yards?

Carefully, Boone moved so that he could get a glimpse of Strongheart's face; he saw the pupils of the dog's eyes, unmoving; Boone followed the line of the eyes -- and found that the animal was staring with intensity not at cars or roads or yards below, but that his sightline was just above the horizon. The dog was contemplating something just beyond vision, deep in meditation of some deeper consequence than people and the city.

Boone is convinced the intelligence of animals is much greater than we realize, that they are capable of deep thought. If this is so, then I ask my students to consider what the human brain is capable of, beyond the degree we use it. Ponder the tremendous potential of observation, blending thought, extra-dimensional thinking and perception.

Dick Kinney taught me much about our minds. It was Dick who had told me back in 1971 that difference between humans and animals, recognizing fully the sensory talents of animals:

"A parakeet has a keener sight than man, a dog has a better sense of smell, and a mink has sharper hearing." He added that if that be so, why is it that man puts the parakeet in a cage, chains the dog in a kennel, and drapes the mink over his wife's shoulders? How can these be?

And Dick's answer remains so significant for the olde English prof -- and for all: "Because man has a better mind. With it he can draw inferences, invent tools, imagine solutions, communicate ideas through written records, and accumulate knowledge through the writings of others."

It all goes back to our ability to think. And thinking is primarily responsible for language. We are all capable of much more than we do, capable of expression, appreciation, perception, awareness. Literature helps in significant measure to bring all of this home to us.

I can't think of any better -- or other -- reason for teaching English.

How many marriages have failed because two ordinary, intelligent people were unable to communicate their hopes, their fears, their dreams to each other? How many hardworking, effective workers in industry have failed to get promotions because, though their ideas were sound, they were unable to communicate them effectively to their superiors?

How many events in the tapestry of humankind have been lost forever because no one at the scene was able to communicate the circumstance so that others might know in later times?

Teaching English is teaching communication. It's the greatest job in the world.

And it is not all nouns and pronouns. Perhaps no experience has brought home that point more than my research into deaf-blind Dick Kinney's remarkable lifetime. He found communication via the movement of the Golden Gate bridge as he stood on that huge suspension structure; music as he touched the steel cables of the bridge. He discerned the attitude of the airliner in which he flew by the pressure on his back as he was in the aisle seat. He knew my height by the angle of my hand and arm as be shook hands, the presence of a photographer by the momentary heat from the flash bulb, the movement of an electric fan in his apartment signalled that someone was pressing the doorbell; and the smell from a bottle of cologne sprayed around the door alerted him once when the fans failed to do the trick -- and worried friends groped for some means of communication.

Memorial Hall was built primarily for basketball games, but there have been memorable programs, dances, and speakers featured there as well over the years. It was there, on a morning some 20 years ago, that I found the full significance of the presence of Dick Kinney.

He had returned to campus to receive an honorary doctorate. Down the steps he came, companion at his side to make sure he didn't fall, guiding him through the pageantry to the stage. And, after receiving the symbolic hood, he then approached the microphone. His voice a bit high-pitched (he couldn't hear) and his step a bit slow (he couldn't see), he drew the crowd to his word, his example.

Free-lance writer that I was, I told Marilyn, "There's a magazine article here." Later I wrote Dick, got his OK for me to come to Winnetka, north shore Chicago suburb, to interview him.

I flew to O'Hare field, rented a car, and thus began a drive to the big city traffic that I would become quite familiar with over the next two years.

"There's a book in all this," I told Marilyn upon my return. "If nobody else is going to do it, I'd sure like to try it."

What a meaningful experience it was! Dick was so cooperative, the others at the Hadley School for the Blind, where he was now President, also helpful. Most of the staff there were without sight, yet all, including deaf-blind Geraldine Lawhorn, helped all they could.

The airlines liked me; I made perhaps five different trips to Chicago in the two-year period I worked on the book -- and learning so much about Dick. Then trips to East Sparta, Ohio, to chat with his mother, then correspondence with a dozen or more persons who knew Dick, many of them former Mount Union students.

In those freshman English classes and in the creative writing classes, I always stress "picture words" -- and yet another application of that approach came in my interviews. Along the way, I interviewed four deaf-blind persons to get a useful perspective on the various challenges and opportunities. And I learned about images.

"If you could have one of the two sensory perceptions back, would you want sight or hearing?"

My question, perhaps, might have seemed a bit harsh, but none hesitated.

"I would want my hearing."

Why? Certainly sight would be so much more helpful! So much more informative!

But I had not thought through things. Each one noted that the sense of touch -- which they had -- could, in some measure, provide information that sight would give. One could, by touch, determine size, shape, texture, placement, etc.

"But there is no other perception that provides for help towards sound."

Dick had told me about putting his hands on the jukebox, feeling a bit of rhythm -- but that was about the only compensating experience he could share.

Through the Rain and Rainbow did not reach any spectacular sales, but I am grateful that Dick's story of achievement over adversity was shared through the several editions of the book. In my professional career, I've included many times an anecdote or two of Dick's life to provide "picture words" for the audience of living up to our potentials as humans.

And his example lives on in many ways.

The woman who came up to me after one of my presentations had tears in her eyes. "Is there any way that I can get a copy of the story about that deaf and blind man?"

"Why, of course." My answer was prompt, efficient.

"It might help." Then she explained. Her son would be coming home the next day, after many, many months of hospitalization. He was now a quadriplegic, the result of an automobile crash.

The woman's tears increased. "He needs -- he needs some inspiration. If I could have him read about Mr. Kinney --"

I gave her the copy I had with me.

If it would help in any way, my day was far more complete now than merely measuring it by the size of the audience, by the amount of the fee, by the applause.

In his poem, *Out of Chaos*, Dick Kinney uses the rainbow to make his point about whether we spend our time regretting what we've missed, or doing what we can and rejoicing. He wrote:

> Does the rainbow in the prism
> As it spreads its laughing beams
> Pine at bitter cynicism
> At the ordinance of heaven
> For restricting it to seven
> Of the colors that it dreams?

And later Dick asks, "Shall a man for what he has not/Stultify the good he knows?"

Of course not. Do what you can, shine with those seven basic colors given the rainbow, let your beauty brighten the sky, enhance the lives of all around you.

Let not narrow view, cynicism, restrictive prejudice dictate your life.

Nashville, Tennessee. Another convention of the National Council of Teachers of English in the 1960s. Three days -- and now the two-hour train ride to Cincinnati and a night ride back home. One passenger car and a diner plus four baggage cars. I sat in the rear, reading a paperback. One hour out, at 9 p.m. the train stopped. It would not resume its journey for another six hours.

But we didn't know that. In fact, the 30 persons in the car were never told -- until panic struck. I became aware as the passengers -- all women -- began to move to the back of the car, a few children began crying -- and loud, obscene remarks ripped through the car.

"He's crazy!"

"He'll come after us!"

One other man -- and he was letting everyone know of his frustrations. The language was frightening. And this English prof, shaken from the drowsy reading of some academic tome, inhaled deeply, soothed the frantic women who now cowered by the rear door -- with no place to go for the train was in absolute isolation now stopped for some 45 minutes without an explanation, somewhere in the vast, awesome hills of Kentucky.

Am I to be a hero? Or will he take out his vengeance on me? His foul language flew everywhere as I approached.

And then, in that troubled year of 1963, when I saw the foul-mouthed one, the entire pattern emerged. I saw a young black man. Perhaps 15 years of age. And every other passenger in the car had seen the color of his skin. And had heard his shouts of confusion and anger.

Oh, those were clear enough. Enough to put the entire car a hair's breadth from utter panic.

But none had seen the other communication.

The white cane at his side.

His first train ride. A simple 2-hour jaunt to Cincinnati where family would meet him. Now, the train had stopped. No porter. No conductor. No one to answer his questions. Wipe away all the dirty words and all he wanted to know was whether this was the station. The long wait, the mounting moments. Would somebody tell me what is going on!

I sat beside him, explained as much as I knew, and knew through the long hours which followed that this young man was not the only blind person on that train.

We were all blind. The communication broke down because race, language, emotion got in between us. How foolish we were!

I think of the importance of an instance when Dick Kinney was on campus as an undergraduate, serving his fraternity as its chaplain. The year was 1953. The story has been passed down to me that Dick and his fraternity brother, John Wilson, were the leading forces behind the local chapter admitting its first non-white to membership. The student was an Iranian, but the lesson carries the same significance whether he had been an African, Chinese or Hispanic. Parvis was, most importantly, the first non-white admitted to the local chapter.

And Dick Kinney, deaf and blind, combined his leadership with John Wilson, born blind, to nominate, endorse, and successfully advocate the admission of Parvis Ami Parvis.

A good lesson for us all.

You and I can emote without language, we can love or fear or hate, we can have gut judgments without language; but you and I cannot philosophize without language. To interpret requires words, symbols of ideas and sequences of the symbols.

"That is why we will have vocabulary tests." My freshman classes fidget at the thought of them. The sun shafts into the basement room; outside there are flagpole rallies and softball games and frisbees, and yet I continue. "Word power is thought power." I am impressed with my sloganeering. The class is restless.

"Thinking is a process of testing and selecting and rejecting words. You take this idea and that experience and put them together. Then you have a host of possibilities, rejecting some words, accepting others."

I make squiggles on the brownboard, some arrows and abbreviations for the words. It will appear totally meaningless the next hour when Prof. Pinney's accounting class meets in the room.

"We've noted that writing takes the same process, a process which always begins with thinking." I draw a circle above a stick-figure head on the brownboard. "Words. You select those which will do justice to your thinking." Words will go in the circle.

"Now; what is the process?" No hands flutter. Then a lanky young man by the door says, "Selection and rejection."

"Good. Selection of what?"

"Words."

"And what if you don't have more than one word for the given thought?"

He shuffles his feet. "Well, you know, you can't do it."

"Can't do what?"

"Like, you know, select."

And somebody chimes in, "Can't reject either!"

"Yeah, you know, that's what I meant. Know what I mean?"

What if American history had been written in 1981? What if Tom Jefferson hadn't put the words on paper for the ideas?

The Declaration of Independence might have turned out like this: "When in the course of, you know, what comes to everybody, it becomes necessary for one bunch of people to, like, really, smash up all the political hands that have, you know what I mean, pushed everything together and, like, it is time to say 'whoa!' Like we got to make it loud and clear. Like we are pushing stuff to be, like, right out in the open. Like self evident. Like, we got some rights, you know what I mean?"

One of the reasons we fall back on "you know" and the other cop-out phrases is that the accompanying nod indicates ready comprehension. We prefer to think -- and assume that others think -- in simple blocks. That great irony in my classes of thinking-writing was that I insisted on specifics, tie-down picture words and precise descriptive words -- and at the same time encouraged abstractions in thought. Thing-thinking is easier than concept-thinking. But we need both.

How many have a concept of what a substitute for thing-thinking might be? J.N. Hook, distinguished lecturer for the National Council of Teachers of English, has said, "If we do not need to think intensively about how to get our next meal, we tend to substitute another thing." Few have insight into thinking about intangibles.

Anatole France put it this way. "The whole art of teaching is only the art of awakening the natural curiosity of young minds for the purpose of satisfying it afterwards."

William James has suggested that wars would end only when we find a "moral equivalent" of war. Man is instinctively competitive; if he doesn't fight wars, he must find something else to combat. Prof. Hook concluded that similarly people must find the equivalent of thing-thinking in order to reduce it. We must show the young that dealing with abstractions, with ideas, is more challenging and rewarding than being exclusively concerned about sports and hot rods and clothing.

A prof does not teach a course on thinking. He teaches thinking in every course in the catalog.

And the students in my creative writing classes kept me well supplied with specific ways the words have meaning. I was urging them to come up with a good slogan for a fast-food restaurant -- something more relevant than "McDonald's" or "Wendy's." The assignment stemmed from a trip to England my family took in 1985 -- and seeing a Scottish equivalent with the name "Gobble and Go."

Well, I gave the assignment -- and expected that some students would have creative responses in a few days, perhaps a week of ponderings. But Ray Camma fooled me. After a moment, he came up with what has to be one of the most efficient names for a truly efficient fast-food restaurant we could conceive.

He said, "How about 'Eat It and Beat It'?"

That I liked!

Or consider the wordplay in 1989, in the final creative writing class I taught at Mount Union. I suggested students work on some advertising slogans which would incorporate references to the *Bible*. Nothing sacred in advertising: And the class came through in great fashion.

One wrote, "Moses Printing Company -- for Those Truly Important Documents!"

And my favorite, a slogan for the exer-cycle: "To Kill the Fatted Calf!"

11

Newshawks -- and a Few Chickens

Alliance, Ohio, is distinguished for a number of reasons beyond my presence. For one, the original Taylorcraft airplane, rage of the 1930s, was manufactured in Alliance during those gala times; for another there is a monument at the local train station commemorating a speech made by President Abraham Lincoln when he got off the train in Alliance in 1862.

Very few persons ever have gotten off the train in Alliance since that time.

But the annual "Carnation Festival" is a yearly time of celebration -- even more so a few years back when a typo cropped up in the local newspaper, the *Review* "The highlight of the Carnation Festival this year will be the drowning of the queen..."

That important link between happening and reporting is one susceptible of many quirks and unexpected paths. It happened occasionally in my journalism classes, too.

The custom developed for Journalism classes (English 230 in the catalog in the 1950s and 60s; later it became Communications 240) to have an unannounced, dramatized news "event" of some sort take place during the term. We had a book burning under the American flag, an insidious attempt to plant poisonous gases under the campus terrain, a mysterious bomb scare in Chapman Hall, the bomb was skillfully defused by Dr. Jim Rodman, head of the Physics department, who ordered everyone to "stand back!" as the bomb fizzled. A little flag popped out saying "Bang." UFO landings, protest rallies, kidnappings -- all have occurred; trumped-up events which always begin with somebody dashing into the journalism class saying "My gosh! Did you see it?" or "Something terrible has happened!"

My student journalists always responded well. Too well on occasion. A secretary was posed as a kidnap victim, bound and gagged in a blue and white car about two blocks from campus...with various clues which, over a half-hour time, took the journalists to that vicinity. Two young men enrolled in the class arrived considerably ahead of the others -- 15 minutes or more -- and found the victim. They pulled the gag from her mouth and asked the journalist's litany of questions. "Who? How did you get here? When? Why?" The secretary carried out her role perfectly, answering their questions according to her script, relieved that at last somebody could get her out of the wrist bindings and gag.

"Thank you!" The two enterprising reporters said -- and then put the gag back in Linda Gray's mouth, rolled up the window, and tore off to the next clue.

It was nearly two weeks before Linda would even speak to me.

But I got my come-uppance in 1976. The "story" for another class was to cover various aspects of a legal case which would develop in class. Pam Creedon, a journalism student of other years and then our public relations director, was to come into the room with a policeman, saying "He's the one who hit my car!"

That, in turn, would lead to the parking lot, assessment of damages, a third party driving by -- and all sorts of story lines to follow.

Pam knew the old prof. Knew his journalism antics. She'd be a good participant. I'd contacted Detective Conway of the local police department -- he'd assisted in many of the other stunts. He'd be businesslike, and so the script was carefully planned. A date picked. The class would not know in advance -- not till that magic moment when I'd be in the middle of a stirring lecture and the door would burst open with the accusation "He's the one -- he hit my car!"

I was in good form that afternoon, basking during my lecture in the knowledge that another perfect dramatized news event was about to go off as scheduled. No need to worry about another one for two more terms. I was relaxed, free.

And the door burst open. Pam entered with Detective Bryce Conway of the Alliance Police Department at her side. Students grew more and more excited in anticipation of that magical, suspended moment of awareness.

And then everything went blooey. Pam did not say the intended lines I had for her. Pointing directly at me, with fear written over her face, she said "There he is! He's the one who did it to me!"

No mention of a "car" at all. Conway dashed to me, put me against the brownboard, frisked me, and kept referring to the horrible professors, the immoral faculty. He pushed, shoved -- while I protested an innocence of heinous crime which I had not contemplated for the story! Oh, they carried out their act beautifully... clear out to the cruiser! I fear that some in the class to this day are convinced their prof had assaulted Ms. Creedon behind some bushes on that fatal autumn day!

Their stories were tough to grade. After the events -- which took an hour to explain -- subsided and they handed in stories, I was still quaking a bit. Conway was laughing -- and Pam was grinning as she kept saying something about "getting even for my grade in journalism four years ago!"

I ended up giving an "A" to everybody. I mean, after all, some papers showed tear stains as they wrestled over a story about the dirty, low-down actions of their maniac prof. How could I acknowledge anything but a valiant, superb effort on their part?

I spent much time dreaming up the fake episodes. In one a librarian was taken hostage by a demented alumnus and held in an office in another building. The graduate demanded that a letter -- a note of considerable defamation of the administration's character -- be printed in the campus newspaper. In another related instance, the class took on my challenge to see whether they could devise a trumped-up story about an unidentified flying saucer. By golly, they ended up with ashes, charred remains of an aluminum foil apparatus, and some gibberish on notepaper -- added it to the exclamations of a few of them that "strange lights" were seen the previous evening just at that spot on campus -- and the whole thing was duly reported in the local press, a story which read like the real thing.

But some people can do better than I with such goings on. In one of my dramatizations for class coverage, I neglected to clue in all whom they might meet. The story concerned the theft of a invaluable tooth from a million-year-old wooly mammoth, the tooth taken from a display case in our science building. A secretary had been alerted to report a strange man in the building earlier that day, all profs knew about the dramatization, and one was set for an interview on the significance of the mammoth.

Another, in a vain attempt to save the tooth, would be found outside the building, beaten by the thief. Down the street a pedestrian was ready to give testimony to a "wild looking man" who was carrying "a large something, looked like a gun" who had commandeered a car to whisk him away. There was more, but I had forgotten about the janitor in the science building -- a man with considerable imagination. When several students asked him about the tooth, he started in on a fabrication of his own much more colorful and lively, I fear.

Why, there had been a hundred people dashing through the building; yep, and they had uniforms on. And the police were there, yep. By cracky, it was a scene all right! Took a dozen away in ambulances. *Ad infinitum.*

There were two sets of papers to grade that evening.

One had the "true" story covered; the others were stories written by the eight or nine students who had encountered the janitor along the way.

Of course, sometimes the journalism stunt got a bit out of hand for other reasons. In 1983 when the Tolerton-Hood Science building at Mount Union was being constructed -- girders up, men working on the lofty steel sections -- I had my friends Rita and Dick Hamilton, active in the community theater, helping. At 7 a.m., I alerted the workmen that the scene would all be fake, of course. This time with a gun in hand, jumping out of a car parked by the building construction, Mrs. Hamilton pretended to be ready to shoot herself, despite the pleadings of her husband. Students had flocked out of Chapman Hall when given the "alert" by a planned interruption in the class.

One problem: the foreman was not at the scene at 7 a.m.... and the workmen did not tell him of my explanation. High above the others, he saw the stunt unfolding and shouted, "Stop that woman!" The foreman started working his way down the girders, shouting and screaming as he saw Rita hold the gun to her head. Students baffled the foreman -- why didn't they intervene? Save that woman's life! They were just standing around, making notes!

I ran over and corralled the foreman just in time. Not a planned part of the story... but a very necessary scene that morning!

Journalism provides a never-ending series of observations to judge the merit of speed communication. When the Bert Lance "scandal" broke during the Jimmy Carter presidency there was a flurry of concerns. Lance had apparently used an airplane for government business, although it belonged to a private bank. In any event, one of Lance's chief antagonists was Illinois Senator Charles Percy, former president of Bell and Howell. Jody Powell, Carter's press secretary, called on a Chicago newspaper and tipped it to a possible violation by Percy -- using a Bell and Howell airplane while on government business.

There's a journalistic term for such a side-door tip. In any event, the Chicago paper, printing the allegations, found out that Bell and Howell didn't even have an airplane. Jody Powell had to apologize for the story possibility. *The Plain Dealer* of Cleveland headed the story with proper terminology -- but the net result just didn't turn out quite the way intended:

>"Jody Caught
>In Percy Leak"

Which may be worse than having to apologize! The headline had to be written quickly, of course. No chance to dally around, philosophize for a day or so, experiment with a variety of phrasings. Journalism teaches the need to meet all deadlines. That's why Sally showed up for J-class one day lugging a tire into the room. And Sally was not a large, muscular girl. She collapsed into the first chair by the door, the tire slamming to the floor.

"What is this?" The class was of a mind to assume the dramatized news event was about to start. After all, we were twenty minutes into the class period by now.

"Look," Sally said, "I had a flat on the way. That's why I'm late. And I knew you wouldn't accept just any excuse. This is journalism." She phrased the last sentence with considerable force.

"But --"

"I brought it along. Proof, old prof; proof that I had a flat tire. Now, can I turn in my story for today without penalty?"

Sally Quinlan went on to be a fine high school journalism teacher. She had learned her lesson well.

"To what lengths a professor will go to train a class!" So wrote Kathy in her creative writing journal. She was enrolled in both that class and my journalism class at the same time -- a fate few could master, I fear. In looking back over her writer's journal from 1965 (she never picked it up on end-of-semester day and I never throw student work away, one of the reasons it was difficult to ascertain whether I was at my desk when one entered the office) I find I perpetrated a vile crime for the journalism class. "Imagine -- even to stealing two paintings from the library just for a journalism exercise!"

Kathy's journal entry was probably right -- maybe it was just an exercise in those days. The class had been taken outdoors that warm May afternoon, strolling by the library on our way to the trees by the campus lakes, there to discuss First Amendment guarantees of press freedom when a man dashed out of the library with two paintings under his arms, shouting "Never again! Never again! Never will anybody have to view these horrors!"

He dashed down steps, through the class and to a waiting car. The librarian pursued, shouting invectives which would do credit to a state university more than a church-related college.

What horrors? Why the theft? "Sounds like a story, folks," I muttered. "Track it down. You have two hours."

With that I strolled back to the office, waiting to see who the student leaders would be that year. Kathy, it turned out, was one of them. Even got an interview with the "thief" at the police station. Bill Krahling, former PR director at Mount Union, and later an executive officer of the national Alpha Tau Omega fraternity, had done his "act" beautifully.

Something about the man's family history and its distortion in two paintings given the college by a demented member of the family. Paintings done by an insane artist. Paintings lauded, however, and proclaimed masterpieces by critics.

Oh, well. How does one define art, anyway?

A student learns in many ways. In journalism, I stressed accuracy -- accuracy--accuracy. That was the slogan of Alfred Ochs, founder of *The New York Times* -- so why not apply it to my classes? And it worked. So much so for one young man in 1987 that it was nearly his end.

The dramatized news event in journalism class that year involved my actress friend Rita coming into the classroom and recalling "sins" of her past as a student, finally putting a gun to her mouth. She then committed suicide, despite the pleas of her husband who then knelt by her body, pleading for life to return. The class knew it was the trumped-up story, of course, with many clues to be unveiled across the campus leading up to this act, yet the acting itself was far more effective, apparently, than might have been suspected. From that opening scene the class dashed out, retraced steps, got the background to the story. Their final copy was due in two hours.

The last student to come in the office with copy was right at the deadline. He was a hefty athlete who placed the story on my desk and shook his head. "Man, that was a *tough* story!"

"You're right at deadline," I noted. "What made it so difficult?"

"Man, I tell you the toughest part was to see this dead woman right there on the floor, and to see her husband crying over her, and then for me to have to go up top him and say, with my notebook in my hand, 'How do you spell your middle name?'"

He concluded, "I mean, like, you know, man, that was hard!"

And who am I to doubt that?

In looking back over the years with journalism students, however, I recall as well those who flinched not when the difficult called -- in "real" situations. Jeff Wason, for instance, had an internship with the *Warren Tribune-Chronicle* in 1985 and was doing general assignments. Learning the on-the-job skills which could be translated into 12 hours of academic credit to conclude his Mount Union experience. I had taught him about leads, headlines, features -- even about checking on the spelling of middle names! But none would really be the final "test" for any reporter. For Jeff it came on a Friday afternoon as he had started driving back to campus for a weekend of partying and unwinding after the week on the job. And he showed then what a true reporter is made of.

On the car radio he heard of a violent tornado striking just a few miles away. Not a trumped-up campus story by the olde prof, but a dramatic, tragic, awesome story unfolding. Skip the plans for Friday night. Jeff drove to the scene, was the first reporter there, captured in words and pictures the dimension of the violence -- and his story made top-of-page in the *Tribune-Chronicle* the next day.

With Jeff's by-line.

And when the *Tribune-Chronicle* a week later did a tabloid summary of the tornado's damage and the accompanying feature aspects, the dimension of human tragedy and yet the outreach and care as well -- it was Jeff's personal remembrance of that Friday afternoon that was the opening story.

You can't teach the motivation to do the job. You can't teach the awareness to forget all the weekend plans. You can tell about them, but it takes personal motivation. Jeff had it. He never got back to campus at all that weekend. The journalist in him was more important than anything else.

On another matter, who knows the inner workings of the mind, say, of a reporter -- an artist in his own right? Who knows how information is captured -- and shared -- when words themselves may not accurately convey information. Each word may be correct, but the synthesis of all in a story may be the work of what might be termed a reporter-artist.

In basic newswriting class we get into the atmosphere of interviewing and news gathering after just a day or two of preliminaries. Might as well jump right into it.

At this point I discuss the gathering of materials -- and accurate reporting. "Never take a notebook with you, never shove a formal spiral bound notebook in front of your interviewee."

"In front of what?" I forgot that they do not understand Latin. "The person you're talking to."

I continue. "Just take a simple piece of paper with you." I draw one from my coat pocket, fold it into sections. "Much less formal this way."

I move towards the class. "Then you ask the questions which become the basis for your story. Mike, do you like the new Dean?"

He is surprised. "I don't know."

"Janet -- do you like the new Dean?"

"I guess so."

"What about you, Ken?"

"I don't know. Maybe."

Moving now to the back of the room. "Is he honest, Marge?"

"How would I know?"

"Do you think he might be a liar on occasion?"

She fidgets. "Maybe. How would I know?"

"Do you like the way he dresses?"

The class snickers a bit. Somebody says, "He's pretty formal."

"Is it good to have formality all the time, Rich?"

"Naw."

"Do you like this college town, Bill?"

"You mean Alliance?"

"Oh, didn't you know the name for sure?"

"Well, yeah. Like it's ok."

I ask more questions, jotting down their scatter-gun answers as I walk through the class. Then I sit down at the desk. "Now I'm back

in the newsroom. I'll write my story. Go ahead and chat a while, do what you wish. I'll have the story in -- oh, in about three minutes."
To make the point I had in mind all along would take no longer. The class is unsure what is going on; they fiddle around, some watch as I get out another sheet of paper and begin to write. The final product doesn't take all three minutes. And, of course, it wasn't worth it, either.
"Here 'tis. From the notes and your comments. A great story, probably feature it tomorrow; lots of controversy." I read:

> The majority of students interviewed at Mount Union College today declared they are unable to admit any public support for the new Dean of the College, despite the trustees three-year-long search culminating in Dr. A.B. Zilch assuming that post a month ago.
> Two-thirds of those interviewed offered no sense of fondness for Zilch.
> Even more disconcerting is the fact that 50 percent of the students believe Zilch is a liar and that his formality, according to some, hurts his rapport with students.
> Students at the College displayed a lack of enthusiasm as well for Alliance, one expressing wonderment that a college would ever locate there...

"Any comments?"
None develop. I raise the question again; finally one says, "That isn't exactly fair -- the way you did it."
"Oh?"
Others are fidgeting again. After all, the integrity of the prof is now in question. This is not the way to achieve good grades in class.
"What do the rest of you think?"
Mostly silence. One young woman learns forward. "Technically, I suppose, it's ok."
"Would you write it the way I have?"
Now she's in trouble. That's what happens when you lean forward in journalism class.
"Well --"
Another interrupts. "No. It's unfair. You didn't get enough sampling. And --"

"And what?"

"Well, you kinda put words in our mouths, I think."

Of course I did. And I took a weak sampling. And the issues were so general they made no sense at all. And the story reflects more a desire to be dramatic than to be honest. It's easy enough to do; two, three minutes and you have startling sentences. But it's worthless.

"Yet, ask yourselves, when a poll is announced on TV or in the papers, how often is the number interviewees given? And then you read in the papers some description of expressions or philosophies, keep in mind how possible it is that it reflects what the reporter wanted, not what the interviewee had in mind."

Then I pick up the current issue of the campus paper and share a paragraph here, another there which reflect this concern. What good are generalized musings without the specifics? What good are guidelines without understanding what may happen if they are not followed?

We have much yet to learn about these issues.

The olde prof retires to his office, though, with a bit of satisfaction.

We now know the meaning of "interviewee". That's a useful -- even if academic -- start!

12

Traditions

In those salad days of mine at Purdue, I learned the engineers' cheer -- something which blended the best of the math books with the Boilermaker's desire to win every ball game they had:

> e to the x, dy/dx; e to the x dx.
> cosine, secant, tangent, sine
> 3-point-one-two-one-four-nine
> square root, cube root, BTU,
> slipstick, slide rule -- yea Purdue!

My office at Purdue was a basement cubicle shared with two others, graduate students; at Indiana U it was a similar cubicle, but this time shared with three graduate students. At Iowa State I had progressed, sharing Prof. W.J. Jones' spacious office, using a converted table along the south wall.

At Mount Union College I started with a room shared with three student assistants and a part-time secretary.

At Mount Union I had no engineer's cheer. but I did find a long history -- 123 years -- of tradition which began back in the mid-19th century with this exhortation:

> Oskee-wow!wow! Skinney wow!wow!
> Skinney wow! wow! Mount Union!

Encountering that, I sometimes longed for good old Purdue. I dipped into Mount history further, and found -- fortunately -- that the following had faded from favor a century before I arrived:

>Wah he/ wah he/ rip zip/ bah ze/
>I yell/ I yell M.U.C.!

We've come, some, from those days. Now it's "Give me an M! Give me an O! Give me a U! Give me an N! Give me a T! What do you have? Mount! Rah, rah, rah!"

All of which is a reminder of the low point several years ago in our college's long history of commencement exercises. A young woman had spent most of her lifetime as a student with us, I fear, finally accumulating enough points to be eligible for graduation. On that hot June afternoon, inside the gymnasium, I know that all faculty members were breathing sighs of relief at the awareness that she was, indeed, going to leave us at last.

"You didn't say it positively had to be in today!" she once had said to me, her theme already three days late.

"I said it would be due the next class period." My remonstrance was surely effective.

"Well, but I didn't come to class for three days -- remember? So this is really just the next class time for me." Her bubble gum popped in my ears. "Right?"

I took the theme, read it that night after growling at the dog and telling Marilyn her homemade vegetable soup was just fair.

But the student was consistent; I'll say that. She had trouble with every class, every prof. Near the end we were giving her passing grades, of course, considering more of her presence not really worth the merits of tenure.

The academic procession was quiet, dignified. We sat there through the speakers, on to the awarding of the degrees. Polite applause whenever a student was receiving one with honors. Everything was orderly until the one in question came to the stage.

As soon as her name was called, a new kind of cheer went up in the audience of some 2000 persons. Heads jerked to the side to identify the cluster of four who stood up, shouting, "Give us a C! Give us an A! Give us an N!...." and so on, ending with "What do you have?" and her name. It was shouted in glorious mayhem by her own parents and family.

President Weber stood in awed silence through the entire showcase, finally offering the coveted degree.

The young lady accepted it; made a victory sign, as I recall. Of course, the President had not positively said it would be given today. It could have been three days later.

But, then, the faculty would have missed the show.

After all, about a dozen of them joined in the cheer!

Mount Union College, my employer for 36 years, has had its share of commencement stories. Like many others, I am sure, we had some seniors who chose to show their concerns for a war they did not understand. One young man, who disdained the conventional robe and who wore well-worn blue jeans to the stage in 1969, later became an attorney identified with the conservative wing of the Republican party.

Whatever happened before Levi Strauss came up with his jeans? Might make a good scholarly paper for someone to undertake. I recall a young woman who did not show up for class, was duly marked absent, and then appeared the next day. "How come you weren't here yesterday?" My question was perfunctory.

"Couldn't come," she said. "I mean, like, my mom washed my jeans! I just couldn't come!"

Maybe somebody could work up a good career dirtying freshly laundered jeans. Might make a million.

My colleague, Dr. Jim Rodman of the Physics Department, is an absolute nut with crossword puzzles -- *The New York Times* and *The London Times* puzzles are his favorites. I can't even read the definitions without getting confused in those two. Jim takes puzzles everywhere -- right into faculty meetings (occasionally looking up to mutter objections to the proceedings) and into commencement exercises. The story is told that when one of Jim's sons was in the line to receive his diploma Jim actually looked up from *The New York Times* puzzle to observe Jeff get the degree -- then back to work on the puzzle.

Commencement serenity has been lost in a variety of circumstances. The date under the three-term system in effect in 1970s and early 1980s was always mid-June -- and the hottest afternoon of the year. I'm sure it reached 130 degrees in the gymnasium. Some years ago, I marched in with all the dignity I could muster, assumed my place in the proceedings, finding that my assigned place was at the end of a 14-chair row. The speaker that dreadfully hot day was an astronaut, though few, I fear, heard much of what he was saying. With suitcoats and ties underneath the heavy academic robes, we were all baking. For those who were seated in the tiers along either side of the gymnasium floor, however, what happened mid-way in the speech must have been the object of considerable curiosity.

I sat there, daring not to move or twitch, lest I collapse under the weight of my own watery self. I became aware of a movement of heads along the row -- something which apparently started at the other end. One head would turn to the right, then to the left, passing along some sort of message. Fire? If not, what kind of emergency? My mind raced ahead.

Finally the message reached the one to my right and he, in turn, passed it along. "Psst." He had my attention.

To understand what followed, one must realize that Mount Union is a Methodist-supported institution with a long and commendable record of support and service. One does not have to be a Methodist to become a faculty member, however, and thus many of us reflect a spectrum of affiliations. It so happens that I was one of the just two then on the faculty who were active in a certain local church which offered, for someone in that commencement row on that hot June afternoon, a basis for an inquiry.

"Psst." I turned in his direction, looking anxious.

"They want to know -- down there -- they want to know--"

"Yes?"

"Can Christian Science do anything about sweat?"

With at least half the audience of 2,000 staring in confusion at the parade of heads turning, I hesitated not at all. "Divine Love is universal in its adaptation and bestowals!" I said. "Pass it along."

Come to think of it, in light of other commencement history, perhaps I should have stood up and said "Give me a C!" Or something like that.

In my final nine years at Mount, I served, by appointment, the role of the College Marshal, a role which involves all the detail work for the exercises, and the opportunity to hold the college mace and lead the procession. It is a privilege and I do it with some dignity, I'm sure. But I do appreciate the fact that I, too, wear the black robe which covers my entire body during the long procession.

You see, I must stand in front of the entire assembled audience as I turn in front of the podium, hold the mace, and watch like some academic traffic cop while everyone files in correct step and placement.

The coverall robe helps my sense of serenity and decorum.

But it was more than a robe which led to my downfall some years later. Still serving as the College Marshal until retirement in 1989 (I'm not sure why; usually the administration appointed a marshal for a period of four or five years, then switched. Perhaps what happened in 1983 tells the story, however) I was serving on a committee to come up with a new mace or symbol for the college.

We'd been using a simple gavel with purple and white ribbons as our symbol. College colors, but not very dramatic. However, few knew that a piece of wood from the original college building in 1847 was in the historical room at the library.

A mace from that original wood! Terrific idea -- and so the head of the art department, Jim Hopper, designed the mace, some 4 feet long, with the lamp of knowledge on top, some other symbolic embellishments, and the original piece of wood as the core of the entire mace.

A fine cabinet maker constructed the mace -- and in the spring of that year I could proudly lead the procession with the classic mace. Two days before commencement, President Ben Lantz called me to his office. "After the degrees are given," he told me, "I'd like you to come forward and hold the mace while I explain its historical significance."

Fine. The day came. I led the procession into Timken gymnasium, 2,000 persons watching in awe and in great respect, I marched to the front... held the mace, then turned and placed it in a fine holder the cabinet maker had fashioned. I sat down. Degrees were given.

"Will the college marshal please come forward." My signal. I strode forward, picked up the mace, and faced the 85 faculty members seated in front of me, the 200 seniors behind them, and the some 2,000 spectators in the stands.

The president began to read a prepared statement -- which probably sounded fine when he read it to his wife the night before. However, standing behind me on the podium, the president began his statement -- and some 2,000 persons roared with laughter.

"Ladies and gentlemen!" The president was in fine voice. "You see before you now a genuine relic of Mount Union College!"

I do not think he ever realized what the implication was. I started mouthing "Not me! This mace!" pointing to the historic piece of wood in my hand.

The president continued his brief statement... but nobody was listening anymore. I had become the authentic, accredited, genuine relic of Mount Union College at that moment.

As I noted before, professorial status can be a very humbling experience.

And beyond the formality of commencement I've had other moments of possible misinterpretation. Consider, for instance, the early 1970s and my dramatic encounter in summer theater.

I was playing the villain in the melodrama *The Drunkard*. My colleague from the political science department, Dr. Tom Conrad, was cast in the role of the brother of the young woman whose social status was perpetually in jeopardy as a result of my villainy. In the key scene I was to fling my cape aside (a black cape, naturally) and approach the young thing in her home, ready to display all rascally force at my command.

"Ah! Me proud beauty! I have you in my clutches now!"

Carol Lloyd, the student proud beauty, would scream and just as I rushed to embrace her (there may be a more descriptive word for such action), Dr. Conrad would rush in, grab me, pull me from that last-moment terror of the attack, and demand that I leave. The proud beauty's uncorrupted status thus remained intact. However, each night of the performance, as we gathered in the green room before the curtain went up, Tom Conrad would insist that he would, that night, delay his appearance on stage.

"Ah! Me proud beauty! I have you in my clutches now!"

The rush. Cape aside, the powerful clutch -- or whatever it was supposed to be. But always with the hope that the political science department would not leave me alone. On the final night he delayed -- perhaps 30 seconds. I never did understand what a "clutch" was before. At least not in public.

Faculty participation in summer theater on campus brought out a diversity of personalities and talents. And back in those days of the 1960s we also had faculty stunt nights, times when we'd let down whatever hair we had, and behave as though we were actually having fun, not as we were in the classrooms.

Bill Rice of the Geology department signed on for the stunt night a bit late; we had no time left for his mime act. "Oh, well, I'll come around backstage anyway," he said. "Just in case."

Dr. Jim Rodman was destined to be one of the main highlights that year, playing his guitar and doing an act about one crazy Russian. It was in the mode of a Tom Lehrer recording with the fast singing of *Nikoloi Ivanovich Lobochevsky* and a complete Cossack outfit, including a large handlebar moustache pasted there just before Jim went on stage. After a long string of lyrics Jim inhaled deeply, to begin the second verse of his Russian nonsense.

But no words came out.

Jim faltered, his guitar strumming then stopped and he looked desperately towards the wings. His lanky body began to slump, but he managed to make it to the curtains. It was there we realized that the handlebar moustache was no longer in place -- nor was it on the stage floor.

"My God! He's swallowed the moustache!"

Jim was gagging by now.

"Do something!"

With considerable awareness that the show must go on, one of my colleagues pointed a finger to Dr. Rice. "Bill -- go in for Jim!"

I had rushed to the Coke machine and gotten a bottle. We began pouring it down Jim's throat.

The audience was still laughing at Jim's antics, presuming them to be part of the act. Bill Rice started his mime routine but glanced anxiously to the wings,

Jim survived. He probably had more hair in his stomach than on his chest -- at least for a day or so.

"This, too, will pass," someone told him.

The faculty on any campus undoubtedly is held in questionable posture by many students. At Mount Union, there may be reason based on the history of old Chapman Hall, the "old main" of the campus. Back in the last century, the top floor of that building housed the college's museum, a room full of historical relics including a flock (bevy? swarm?) of stuffed gorillas. For these the college was quite famous. However, the gorillas were disposed of some years before the building was remodeled -- and faculty offices moved to the top floor. Alumni, as you might expect, insist, when returning to the campus, that the gorillas remain on the top floor of good old Chapman

Hall.

Well, some freshmen may hold such opinions, too. Or it may be that at times everything seems to be summarized by a sign posted by the elevators in the newly remodelled building. I approached it one morning, set to go to my office on the third floor.

Affixed to the wall adjacent to the elevator door was the sign, placed there by maintenance workers:

"The third floor is out of order."

I noticed students nodding vigorously as they passed by.

You have the campus-sponsored newspaper. Student fees help to support the costs. The staff reaps little more than a learning experience plus satisfaction -- and the laments of others who feel they've been misquoted or mistreated in the paper.

The spin-off, "illegitimate" papers may come. Heralding an era of protest on the Mount Union campus in the early 1960s was *The Gadfly*. Good name. As advisor to the campus paper -- the "legitimate one" -- I was curious. I checked around the various print shops in town to see if any had done the mimeographing for *The Gadfly*, full, as it was, of nasties about the administration, faculty, and campus customs. All of it anonymous, thus adding spice and flavor to the very idea of competition to the establishment.

Next issue. The old prof made the lead story -- in poetry, no less:

> It was Mr. Crist
> who checked the list
> of printers
> to see who might
> have seen the light

Well, now! That's about as bad a public image as I'd had since the early 1950s when I taught high school ever so briefly. Pictures of Adolph Hitler had been placed, unknown to me, behind the American flag in the journalism room where I held forth! It was Student Government Day, with student policemen rushing into the room, exposing the evidence (which they had placed there the night before) of my treasonable ways, and trundled me off to the local jail.

It all prompted a good laugh, and, now once again I was

something akin to Hitler's authoritarian ways.

The anonymity continued (I had no success in my list-checking) for the duration of the editor's years at Mount Union. Paul Beattie became a Unitarian minister in Indianapolis, author of many tracts on religion and philosophy.

He was a doer.

And he knew people with private mimeograph machines. Or did know them. Which is more than I did!

You're in a class known as "Mass Media." History, legalities, ethics in journalism. A fellow bearded colleague team-teaches it with you, Chuck Morford, the specialist in electronic journalism, I in the print media. And the question is invasion of privacy. You talk about it at length, cite historical cases.

"Photographers take pictures with extremely long-range cameras. Suppose you're in a roof garden and one snaps you across the way -- from another block. You're slopping your coffee, or maybe taking a sun bath on your own roof."

The class points out that this is a time of liberality. "Sure, it's poking around a little bit, but that's the price you pay." Nods from all.

"Should we have any limits -- strictly from an ethical point of view?"

John is emphatic. "A long-range camera doesn't mean anything. I mean, like, if you're out there, wherever, you're fair game."

"What about a reporter posing as, say, a teacher?" I had given them the case of the *Albuquerque Journal* in 1981 sending a reporter into the classroom under guise of a substitute teacher. She had the necessary teaching credentials -- but the school did not know she was working as a reporter, actually on assignment in the schools.

"That's up to the schools to handle," Jean said. "You have to be open about these things."

"What if I were not really a prof -- but a news reporter from some magazine, investigating classroom discipline or student achievement. Wouldn't you object?"

"Sounds great to me." They nod again.

"What if I said something about you personally?"

"Like what?"

"Like you're an impossible student. Lazy. Unmotivated."

"Might be true."

"Would you want me to say it in the story?"

"Not really."

"But you are lazy. Unmotivated?"

"Yeah. I guess. As long as the folks send the money, I'll keep showing up."

"Are you learning anything here?"

He laughs, enjoying the spotlight. "Maybe a little. But you know, it's a drag. This place."

"Want me to tell your folks you feel that way?"

"Not really."

Everybody is relaxed, listening to one of those unrehearsed expeditions into personal analysis which so frequently come up in a classroom. Get on the right side of the student, let the student know you're not going to take it out on his grades. Kind of a buddy-buddy rapport and everybody understands. Classroom by-play.

"What were we talking about?" Apparently I'd lost the focus of the discussion for the afternoon.

"Privacy. Cameras and stuff."

I grinned. "Oh, yes. Well, it was a good discussion. Shall we go through it again?"

They were puzzled. I repeated the question, adding, "Want to discuss it further?"

Then I took out the mini cassette from my coat pocket, laid it on the desk, and switched the "play" button. As soon as that five-minute segment ended, I suggested I play it for John's family. Then I wouldn't have to worry about the charge of being misquoted, would I?

Cassettes have long-range abilities, too. I know no better way to teach that than by allowing the classroom to become a bit of a living demonstration. Preach the gospel, yes, but always supply the specific examples and illustrations to illustrate whatever the gospel, whatever aspect of the gospel you had in mind for that class session.

13
Everybody's Doing It

An elderly slave, one of the cast of characters in *Uncle Tom's Cabin*, was told that he was now free. The old slave pondered a moment, then said, "Them's good words -- but who says 'em?"

A good point. The words are important; who says them and for what purpose -- this is perhaps as important as the words themselves. So professors grumble about the linguistic tepidness of their students, forgetting that beyond the classroom there are examples enough to keep the English department busy. We've had a large pharmaceutical firm asking nationwide, "How do you spell relief?" then giving "R-O-L-A-I-D-S" as the answer.

I can tell you this with confidence: none of my freshman classes were ever that mixed up!

With equal confidence, I can report that I just committed a grammatical goof in the previous sentence. Well, I'm in good company; Thurgood Marshall of the United States Supreme Court has "none" likewise a plural in one of his official decisions, noting that "none of the cases are to the contrary."

Euphemisms -- those bland substitutions for sharper words and phrasing -- can be worse than spellings and structure. The U.S. Energy Research and Development Administration refers to the neutron bomb as a "radiation enhancement weapon."

And every professional athlete interviewed on network TV has said, "Well, like, we gotta go out there, you know, and do a job next half, you know what I mean?"

The best single step we could do to improve radically the language proficiency throughout our nation might be to pass a law banning professional athletes from having informal discussion on the electronic media!

But talk about double meanings! A half-page ad in one of our metropolitan newspapers announced, "Yes! We have fly-button Levis!" Below this was the further information, "Open tonight till 10!"

A newspaper reported a fire which raged all night at Miller's Ice House. By morning, the reporter wrote, all the ice "had been reduced to ashes."

The New York Times described a noted playwright as "a lifelong native of New York."

Back to the euphemisms, or whatever the following might be called; let's just say it was enough to make me wish I hadn't tuned in the Cleveland area TV news. As the Christmas holiday season approached, the executive in one of the area post offices reported to the inquiring newsman that things were going well enough. "Excess sortation has not impacted on us as yet."

I'm a dangerous driver; on the highways I know all the rules, obey signals, even adhere strictly to the 55 mph limit (which can also be dangerous); but at times I almost go through the guard rails, when the radio is on and I hear the crazy things supposedly intelligent people say. "How important is the game coming up tomorrow night, coach?" Radio station near Youngstown, Ohio, I on the Ohio turnpike, cruising and listening.

"Well, I'd say that this is one of those games you're going to have to win," the coach muttered, "if you're going to go through the season undefeated."

Somehow I managed to get back on the highway after that profundity, then switched the dial -- and picked up the radio preacher going full blast about how modern inventions are all a signal of *Bible* prophecy being fulfilled. Trouble was, however, he didn't quite get the right word in his punch line.

"The invention of the printing press has now enabled us to *decimate* the news to everybody at one time!"

There are a few persons, of course, who, having concerns about the media, would tend to support the preacher's contention. But "decimate" means to kill; the word he meant, was "disseminate." To spread around.

The assassination attempt on the Pope in 1981 was broadcast over the Mutual Radio Network with its newscaster noting that "a fuselage of gunshots rang out in Vatican Square today..."

Unless the gunman was in an airplane's belly, I think "fusillade" was the better term.

I've been pondering the results of a study on English competency by an educational group. In the final report, it was noted that "nearly one-half of the students perform below average."

Profoundly redundant -- but sounds terribly important. In fact, it says nothing -- except that in ordinary circumstances, with some other educational group in charge, one would assume that exactly one-half would perform below average. Isn't that how "average" is defined?

Several years ago the Ford Motor Company, Lincoln-Mercury Division, was required to provide seat belts by law. This step was described in a company flyer as a "mandatory option."

I recall an advertisement in one of the Ohio newspapers which spoke highly of the labor-saving devices which the Maytag Company offered -- the ironers, dishwashers, dryers, etc. The half-page ad, attempting, I presume, to suggest that if husbands would buy their wives these products the wives would have longer lives, read as follows: "Men! Don't kill your wives! Let us do your dirty work for you..."

Now, either that was extremely creative, or it was an unfortunate choice of words. Ditto for the mortician's association which announced in a pamphlet that "we have rigid standards!"

And I shared with my basic writing class the Vicks ad which suggested a dilemma for all of us. The punch line was "So try Vicks 44 cough syrup... you'll never get any better!"

I suggested we write themes on why, then, anyone should ever try the syrup if the odds were that bad.

We had more fun with a local wedding story which noted that "the bride wore a white chantilly lace gown which fell to the floor..." Some in the class wanted to know just when it fell.

Perhaps you do not have to revere language to use it correctly, but a little respect for the other person's state of the art might help. Take the case of a lady residing in Lyndhurst, Ohio, who received a letter from the Savings and Loan one day. In flat, no-nonsense computer language, the letter said, "This will advise you that the above mortgage had a call date of June, 1970. Under the terms of the note a balloon payment was due on that date..."

I had a survey course in bookkeeping one time, but I just don't recall the definition of either "call date" or "balloon payment." The first sounds very much like a street walker's offering and the second is obviously full of hot air. Not so with the Savings and Loan, though; and I suppose we're to be able to figure out the jargon.

By comparison, poetry doesn't come out as difficult at all.

Some years ago, after being inundated with appeals to subscribe to *TV Guide* -- more than four years of such regular postal appeals -- I succumbed and filled out the form, awaited my first delicious issue. It didn't come.

What did come was a postcard on which was this message:

"Thank you for your recent subscription to TV Guide. However it cannot be entered at this time inasmuch as we are in the process of converting to a new, more efficient computerized subscription system which will insure better processing of your order."

I think this is known as Murphy's Law... or something even worse.

Even a staid and trusted outfit such as American Heritage Publishing Company can create a bit of chaos with a lack of clear communication -- or perhaps it's merely the fault of a well-meaning underling. In any event, I received all the usual inducements to jack up my business with *American Heritage*; our children were in their grade school years and the American Heritage Junior series seemed a good buy. A year's subscription for six books. Some of the titles shown on the brochures appealed, but *Fur Trappers of the North* just didn't make the grade with us. So, when the renewal time arrived I wrote the publisher -- a Mr. James Parton who, I have no reason to doubt, was a real, actual person. His name was on all the advertising literature and the "personalized" appeals. I asked what titles would be forthcoming for the year. I wrote again. And again. Never had an answer. But a comment did finally filter down from an employee in Marion, Ohio, where the warehouse was located.

"I am sorry, but we do not know what titles we are to publish until they come from the printer."

I was impressed; now I began to realize the full power and authority of the International Typographical Union! Editors gave way to these composing room stalwarts who made all the decisions. I presumed, further, that in the next sequence would be titles such as

The American Heritage Book of Otto Mergenthaler or *The American Heritage Book of Serifs and Column Rules*.

I trust that another aspect of the dilemma will emigrate into the pate of Superior Savings. And while that is happening let us consider the predicament of the district attorney in Corpus Christi, Texas. The Judge there quashed one of the attorney's indictments because it accused one Winston Teeter of exercising control "over property other than real property, to wit: mone of the United States of America...".

Faulty, the Judge said, pointing out to the district attorney that "money" is definitely spelled with a "y."

So, there are times when mechanical proficiencies count. *The Chicago Tribune* carried a story of the dismissal of 42 drug charges against an area physician. The official charge was that he illegally dispensed an amphetamine called "phendimetrizine." The charges, however, misspelled the word, calling the drug "pheudimetrizine." The misspelling was later corrected in the law books, but the physician's attorneys won acquittal, arguing that the original misspelling created a legal ambiguity; the misspelling, indeed, could have meant there were two totally different drugs involved.

Back on our campus, the local newspaper carried the story of a man arrested for "threathening." Now, "uttering and threatening" is a legal offense, but I haven't met a fellow yet who has been successfully prosecuted for "threathening." Noting the misspelling (it appeared three times in a four-paragraph story) in my journalism class, I offered to make time and space available for any student who might wish to step forward and illustrate "threathening" in front of the class. Nobody took me up on it -- although several suggested we cancel class and research it in the snack bar.

Journalists, lawyers, advertising managers -- all handle the language well, but the exceptions merely point out the need to be experts. Our thinking is molded by such persons. And there are times when I might prefer a simple misspelling to the convoluted reasoning in some advertisements. For instance, the Franklin-Simon ad which said "The young individualist has the 'with-it' look today..." How can you be an individualist and at the same time strive to be "with it" in fashion?

Consider the nearby automobile agency which pledged in wide-ranging broadcasts that it offered a "100 percent limited warranty" on all its used cars. Ha!

Or the motel ad I noted in an airline magazine, calling attention to its gala honeymoon suite at $79.50. Below this the ad said, "Extra person in room, $10 each." The poser here is not linguistic in nature -- but still fascinating.

Everything pales when you realize the million dollars the National Broadcasting Company spent, years ago to create the color "N" logo for TV identification. A million dollars for an "N" leads to all sorts of possibilities. Three of my students were ready with a colorful orange "C" for CBS and one has perfected a massive red "A" for ABC. I have told him, however, that it may resemble Nathanial Hawthorne's scarlet letter a bit too much.

"And you know what Hester Prynne did to deserve that one, " I reminded Hal.

"Yeah, but ABC won't have to wear this one on its chest."

"Bosom." That was Hawthorne's term.

"Whatever. It ain't allowed on TV anyway."

Probably not, but the royalties intrigue me.

Cleveland, just 60 miles north of our campus, has gotten more than its share of bad publicity, starting with the legends of the Cuyahoga River -- so dirty a fire actually burned on its surface -- and continuing through a string of bad politics, buildings and sports teams.

However, I think a Pennsylvania newspaper rubbed in the image more than necessary when it headlined a story "Bank Robber Sentenced to 20 Years in Cleveland."

And in Chillicothe, Ohio, in the southern portion, I found, via the area press reporting a violent storm which passed through prior to my arrival, that "several trees were reported blown down by sheriff's deputies." Now, in freshman English at Mount Union we'd say "That, class, is a meandering modifier -- a chunk of the sentence in the wrong place."

Though I don't care for this next one either, I think I see what the dilemma was with the student who wrote a theme about her first airplane ride. Apparently the air was a bit bumpy that day because she wrote, "I sure was glad to get back to old terra cotta again!"

Occasionally little one-page collections of dum-dums in expression make the rounds. When someone mimeographs such a set, I usually end up with a half-dozen copies -- furnished by former students who write little notes saying, "Thought you might be interested in this!" I am, though I suspect some of the "actual" dum-dums may come from some linguist's mind which is having a good time. The accident reports, for instance, culled from many police reports: "A pedestrian hit me and went under the car," and "I collided with a stationary truck which was coming the other way."

And the church bulletin items: "The next fund-raising project will be for new carpet in the sanctuary. All those wishing to do something on the carpet get your paper from the pastor." And "The font is now completed at the south side of the sanctuary; children will now be baptized at both ends."

Or the sports page which told of a basketball player who stayed in the entire game despite a pulled stomach muscle. "He showed a lot of guts doing that," according to the reporter.

But word meanings change. When I recently saw a headline in the campus paper regarding our women's basketball team, I enjoyed a hearty laugh over its ambiguity:

"Veterans Will Spark Female Cagers"

But when the headline went up on my bulletin board in journalism class, I had no students laughing -- not even snickering. "So?"

"So 'spark' has a double meaning." I continue chuckling. Until I realized that "spark" is not used by the current campus set in that context. You don't "spark" anymore; you "make-out" -- or whatever else current jargon calls for. I was merely showing my age by my intrigue with the ambiguity.

Just as people have varied lives, successes, span of years, so do words. And just as personalities build, so do meanings and implications of those 650,000 words we use. I try to recover some of my professorial leadership in class after being unappreciated for the basketball headline. "Go back several hundred years," I tell students. "Not all who left Europe for what was known as the new world in the 1500s and 1600s were looked upon as heroes. Far from it. They were considered by most as dummies. In Holland one who left would be called a 'John Cheese' -- a term of derision."

"But in the Dutch 'John' had the pronunciation of 'Yawn' and 'Cheese' came out more like 'Kaase.' " Then I eyeballed the class. "Yawn Kaase. Now just leap ahead to the 1900s."

They worked at it. "Language fluctuates. Like people. Some change personalities over the years. Others may never change. Yawn Kaase."

"What are you driving at?"

"Just keep pronouncing the words. Bend them a bit--as they were over the years, particularly in the New England area."

Finally, I said, "Where would Mickey Mantle have been without those words?"

I was sure that would do it -- but again I merely showed my age. Mickey Mantle, even in the '70s, was not an appropriate reference. I picked up a sports page from the bulletin board, hurriedly glanced through the baseball scores.

"What would Greg Nettles have done without those words?" Then they caught on. And I learned about changing words, too.

14
Meet God

His office was on the third floor, a chickencoop at the landing, so small he never closed the door; there had to be enough air to ensure breathing. His classes were small, and much of his teaching was by individual conference. I'd enter University Hall adjacent to the mathematics building and Coulter Hall, the biology center, feeling a bit foolish to be going to a writing class rather than some much more sophisticated electronics laboratory or structural research seminar. Everybody else in the house knew they would be engineers; I was in a definite minority at Purdue University, unsure of how science and art would mix in my career.

Emerson Sutcliffe could tell when I was coming; the old wooden stairs creaked more than my nerves in anticipation of what always turned out to be an all-out attack on my writing abilities. He used a bold black pen to mark up my short stories; there was an abundance of such pens on his cramped desk, stacks of manuscripts everywhere. The radiator steamed throughout the winter term, pouring out heat, but he wore a double-breasted coat -- buttoned every time -- and poured out more steam with each critical comment.

Once in a while he would like the stuff I wrote. He'd let me know, perhaps a bit grudgingly, but whenever it happened I would leave as though lofted on clouds down the stairway. Trouble was, I couldn't share my rising star with my fellow engineers who knew of "plot" only in political intrigue and "character" as a 35-year-old civil engineering prof, unmarried, who attended a sex seminar planned for the seniors.

I never thought of Prof. Sutcliffe as a god -- more, perhaps, as the devil's advocate. But a quarter century later it was my creative writing class -- complete with small group discussions in the office -- and time to read the mandatory daily journals. I collected them about every three weeks, checking for insights, intrigues, poems, story ideas, descriptions, assignments which comprised the individual journals. The student wrote some thing I would never have contemplated in my assignments for that third-floor cubby hole.

"This class bores me. Creative writing it isn't." If honesty counts, she'll rate an "A." Maybe I shouldn't read further -- one gets that feeling. Perhaps it is the creaking stairs returning.

"It's this business of ripping people apart. It's Prof. Crist playing God in his own way."

God? With tweeds? Degree from Backhand University, a bicycle, and staring at the girls' knees?

"You're cruel. You think I'm a nothing. I sometimes hate you. But then again I love you. Yes, I love you, too." I continue reading. "I will never be a writer. My writing is me and that's how it will remain. I won't change anything about me. "

Thus endeth the entry. The candor is encouraging, even if the philosophy may be disturbing. What does a teacher of creative writing do? Drill? Scheme? Does the teacher have the right (obligation?) to interfere with the student's modes of writing?

Thousands scan the advertisements regularly, eager for new workshops or conferences on creative writing. They flock to the New Hampshire hills, the Nebraska prairies, the Florida Keys, the California coasts to spend a week with guest professionals. They hang on every word. They make wide notes, nod approvingly. They pay big money for the opportunities. And what can the professionals give in return? Nothing except their own experience. Their own attempts, their successes and failures, their insights and awarenesses.,

That is all any prof can give. And if the student chooses to ignore all the experiences, there is really no need for anyone -- college student, high schooler, adult, senior citizen -- to invest in any way in writing courses.

Observe and interpret. I can share my observations, my elaborations -- and through them I can assist others to be more alert both to what is seen and how to treat it. The maid at a Holiday Inn where I stayed recently said, "All men who smoke pipes are intelligent and all people with adenoid problems are slow -- and all maids in Holiday Inns are frustrated." She intrigues me; she observes, interprets -- even though she over-generalizes; still, she is sharp, specific -- and that is where writing begins. If my journal-writer wishes not to be alerted, there is little need to continue the course.

I lecture (I may be dull, but there can be specificity even in that!), I give illustrations, examples from others, I involve the class in activities designed to stimulate. Sometimes for my own gain, admitted.

"A group of bankers and savings and loan officers in Seattle has asked me to speak to them," I share such information without hesitation. "Now, I'm to talk on creativity among other things. This is a creative writing class -- so you need to get involved. Bankers. I want to suggest to them some good, solid, creative slogans for their business, the handling of monies. Put your creative minds to work, and let's have slogans for them." I start to go on to other matters, when John interrupts:

"You mean, something like 'Jesus Saves?' "

My day is complete. We have blended Christianity with commercialism, two in one. I think Robert Frost would be pleased!

The mode of reference is pertinent beyond that day. This business of the prof playing God; do I hand down the ten commandments of creative expression? Do I merely get the would-be writers together to tell each other how great they are? Shall we sip tea and discuss carbon paper and manila envelopes?

If there is no point of skills reference, if I do nothing more than preside over a mid-morning social hour, is anybody's tuition wisely spent?

But the key to the entry from the student's journal is, again, "My writing is me... I won't change anything about me?" How grateful I would be if students held to such a sentiment when confronted with all their peers who insist on changing personalities with each party night on or off campus.

I do not work to change anybody's personality, but I do hope to make all aware of the broadened opportunities they have to do better justice to their personalities. Superficial observations, lazy phrasings, vague generalities warp personalities far more than one prof who prods students to get a better handle on everything around them.

I pounded the brownboard, dramatizing a point. "Try force! Deliberately try to get more forceful." I pounded in cadence now. "Repetition. 'Of the people, by the people, for the people.' That's one of the reasons it worked. Who in here likes rock music?"

Every hand went up. I started a cassette, some nasal-twang singer with a group called The Grateful Dead or the Rinkydinks or the Dangling Participles or something else. But it had rhythm! Tremendous rhythm. Rock does that. Everybody started tapping. It was repetitious. Most rock is. Some simple melody over and over again. Nothing bland. No uncertain, vague melody. I may prefer ballroom music, but I cannot deny the sharpness and intensity of rock.

"Your poem, Bill; 'These days/ these ways, hamper/damper/me/ and I search/ endlessly/for more...' I can read it with rhythm, but the next step is sharpness. What ways?"

"Well, you know, things that hassle all the time."

"What things?"

"Anything."

"Are you saying that anything -- everything -- is wrong?"

"Not really. But it happens."

"Give me an example of what happens."

"The reader can supply his own."

"I can do that, Bill, without ever having to read your poem."

"Yeah, but the poem says I search."

"How do you search?"

"Well, you know, I keep trying to find something better."

"Better than what?"

"Than whatever is hassling. Man, you know."

The class fidgets again. We wear out blue jeans quickly in creative writing. Four students, however, are yawning. Three are upset at the prof and two are laughing. Some are doodling in their journals. Some write, "Here we go again."

Should I try to change my poet, Bill? Change his value system, his outlook on life, his problems with the hassles? Of course not. I couldn't do this even if I wanted to. I have no idea what is bothering him. I never will know. Not until he tells me; I'd be happy even if he told me without a creative expression.

But soon we terminate class and trot off to the campus center for some Twinkies and drink.

God looms again at the next session. I am God, at the desk. Staring at 21 students and we are reading poems and a young man is reading his poem about shoes. He had been wearing steel workers' shoes when he was a high schooler; metal tipped, heavy shoes. His poem speaks of seeing, for the first time, a steel worker at his labor and realization that wearing the shoes was not just for fun anymore.

The poem concludes noting that he has now purchased new shoes for sport -- patent leather shoes this time.

"The realization; it evokes some philosophical response."

"Sure."

"Do we philosophize in long lines or short ones?"

The class is restless again.

"Maybe long ones."

"Then you have justified your lengthy segments. So, you bought new shoes."

"Yeah."

"Why did you say 'patent leather shoes?' "

A girl screams. A genuine shrieker, rattling the windows. "Why do you keep playing God!" Lynn is the one who spoke of me in such lofty terms in her journal. Everyone is startled. "You're always questioning our words! Why can't you leave it alone! Just let it be whatever he wrote!"

No graduate school study taught me how to handle these situations. Before I can comment, the hysteria moves her to continue. *"Just let it alone!* He said what he wanted to say!"

The young man who wrote the poem is looking at me. Unsure.

My lips purse. "No, I am not God. Not quite."

"Then just let it alone!"

Lynn is crying now. I dismiss class. It will do no good to make her emotional outburst more difficult by arguing, nor by continuing the awkwardness of the moment. I mention something about tomorrow's assignment and we depart.

There was reason for asking about the use of the phrase "patent leather shoes." It was a good reference -- and I was pleased to leave it alone. I just wanted everybody to see the lesson. The young man did not say that he tossed aside those put-on steel-tipped shoes which he thought were in good sport for just "some other kind of shoes." Instead he was specific and sharp. He went for patent leather shoes -- as far opposite as he could get from the steel workers shoes. The specificity underlines his changed viewpoint.

A good reference.

I wanted them all to see how good it was.

Not how bad.

Paul Williams refers to creative writing as an act of controlled daring -- something akin to the base runner attempting to steal home; it will be dangerous, but if he does it just right, if he dares to, it will be worth the effort. He may lose, but the effort is what makes the game worthwhile. Williams adds another danger: "Poetry has the quality of the third base runner racing home while the third base coach is yelling for him to go back, then sliding in safely."

And e. e. cummings wrote that "my father moved through dooms of love..." Is that a dumb misspelling? a wrong word? Or a delightfully creative way of telling the story?

Years ago I found myself on Euclid Avenue in downtown Cleveland, reading my poetry to a noon-hour gathering in an open mall area. I accepted the invitation by the Cleveland Poetry Project because, frankly, I'd never tried holding an audience under such circumstances. Passers-by made their judgment of what I did, but I keep thinking of the little jazz combo which preceded me that hour -- and their final number which was, the leader said, "about poetry." With good tempo surrounding him, the leader took one-syllable words, strung them together, something approximating this:

> It is June and there is a moon,
> you are nice, you have no vice,
> here today, I got my pay, what do you say?
> See the sights, all day and night,
> don't make no pun, just have some fun.
> The day is here, so have no fear,
> you got the time, then be sublime...

Oops! Got a two syllable word in there. By mistake. Oh, well; is this poetry? Is this creativity? Is it a dumb phrasing? Or a delightfully creative way of telling a story?

What should my role be? I know what Sinclair Lewis once said that he would have been a much better writer if he hadn't had a teacher of writing along the way. Mark Twain, not one to be timid regarding his viewpoints, put it this way: "Soap and education are not as sudden as a massacre, but they are more deadly in the long run."

After all, we have now progressed to the point where the computer can spew out "poetry" about as readily as we humans can. At the Yale Computer Center the IBM-7094-7040-DCS computer was linguistically primed with programs written in something called SNOBOL 3 to provide free verse poetic images. Here is what was created, something the IBM-7094-7040 DCS has titled *Meditation*:

> O poet
> Blush like a rotted skin

Brighten like a dusty tower
Dream like an enormous flood;
Tremble like a red locomotive;
Flop like a damp gate!
Let the worth of your odor
Be twitched;
Let the work of your bed
Be stilled;
Let the tautology of your arm
Be reddened;
Let the way of your hat
Be dissolved.
Though all windows rave
Though all costumes reap,
Sweetly, steamily,
Reap, 0 poet!

Shall the prof not only play God but play computer-mechanism repairman as well? Is this what the academic future holds?

Several years ago a gentleman wrote me, wanting to discuss a major writing project. He came to the office, and after small talk about the coyotes adorning the shelves, said, "I know my idea will sell."

"What's the focus of the proposed novel?"

"The Civil War. Can't beat that, huh?"

"Well, what aspect of it?"

"The war. You know, the Civil War."

This fine person who had not written a novel now proposed doing the entire war. My thought went to Don Robertson whose first novel was also about the war. On leave from his journalism assignments in Cleveland, Don visited the museum at Gettysburg, became intrigued with three coins on a glass shelf and the notation that they had been removed from the boot of a young Confederate soldier who died during Pickett's charge. Now, what was in that soldier's mind that day when he put the three coins inside his boot? Why there?

One soldier. One intrigue. And Don's first novel -- titled *Three Coins* -- was his interpretation. I could not convince my new friend: however, that he was attempting too great a scale for his first writing venture.

Learning focus and the range of our potential is a hard lesson. In so-called creative writing it is too easy to repeat the cliches and to offer the pleasant generalities.

"Live a full life!"

"Reach for the stars!"

Yes, I know that Longfellow wrote, "Life is real, life is earnest!" -- and got away with it. Still, the prof admonishes again and again in creative writing, "Show me one life that is full, show me one person in one situation reaching for the stars, show me one meaningful reward." And there are many of my students who conclude I do not believe there are such things -- because I keep asking for proof.

And some in creative writing classes will see the connection between the patent leather shoes and the directness of a Civil War scene; some, however, will ask, "If you really want specifics, why not have the poet say 'I then bought a pair of shoes as opposite to the steel-tipped ones as I could find'' -- which is the point to it all -- instead of being indirect, ironically, by being merely specific?"

I think the answer lies in the recognition that the mind working is what counts. When President of Harvard, Derek Bok said that, among the several qualities of the mind, a "tolerance for ambiguity" is important, a tolerance which arises from the "realization that many problems produce a variety of respectable opinions rather than a set of right and wrong answers."

This is certainly applicable to social issues; and it has relevance to the entire process of creative expression, always making higher demands on our thought.

That is why it endures. Perceiving answers is more lasting than receiving them.

A creative expression grows, matures each time we ponder it. Joe McLaughlin has a poem expressing this perpetual chase between writer and idea; he compares it to a flower and the photographer. Just as the camera is in final focus, the flower growing incessantly, is once again out of focus. We can never snap the shutter at a final, no-movement moment.

Creative writers, aware of the eternal focusing, move to comparisons rather than direct statements. A raised eye-brow, after all, can say more by indirection than all the flowery phrases.

Remember Excedrin headache #4? That was the one on television showing the pained individual with the amazing forehead which opened up revealing a pounding hammer at work. Somebody was probably paid tens of thousands of dollars to dream up that one -- and who is to deny the effectiveness of the graphic picture of that hammer if one feels something comparable?

The commercial maker probably had a college degree. That worries me, for it suggests that only intellectuals can come up with convincing comparisons. But go back to that concentration camp in Czechoslovakia during World War II. One of the children wanted to share the woe of the headache that she and others had, knowing their fates. She wrote, "The heaviest wheel rolls across our foreheads..."

No advanced writing course, no classroom discussions of creativity; but she had the picture words. A picture as graphic as any commercial writer could dream up. "The English language is tough enough and brawny enough and nimble enough..." Whitman wrote. And so, too, was the German language.

All of us use poetry. Muhammed Ali is a jingle-writer, but at least he recognizes what word patterns can be expressive. His fists produced more money (and talent) but the words are part of his personality, too.

The entire concept of what that magic word "creativity" means is an area of suspicion, I suspect. I've taught it at high school, college and professional levels and continue to gain insights. Mike Vance speaks to audiences nationwide on the topic, referring to the dynamic creativity of Walt Disney, for whom Vance worked. He tells of Disney's ability to see through problems and to maintain a posture of confidence and optimism; these are ingredients of the creative process. Writers speak of awareness, double meanings, hidden purposes and symbolisms in their stories. We teach of these.

Back 20 years ago, in a writer's journal for my class, Ed March wrote "I am shackled by restrictions on my creativity ever since I first tried wood sculpture on the backyard sapling." He added, "It still has no bark!"

The scars we leave are sometimes long and unyielding. Yet without the scars at all, there would be no explorations.

Later Ed wrote, "I hope I can return in a few years and tell you that you did not sweat over my inanities for no good reason."

What inanities? A few poems which did not read well? Perhaps. Some attempts at new phrasings? Perhaps.

Tom Minifie 20 years ago wrote in his journal for my class:

  I am no poet
  and I know it!

The more I ponder the teaching of creative expression, the more I come to question judgment of the final products. Maybe I'm all wrong in discussing a student poem, a student story. Maybe what I should do is concentrate on the elements without the final product; it will be manifest and grow in due time. The experimentation with forms, phrases and ideas -- perhaps that is all that counts.

When asked how he got to be a superstar, baritone Sherrill Milnes, according to an interviewer, "doesn't even mention voice. He talks about desire, commitment, believability, stemming from internal conviction, about a drive to communicate."

Long before the public performance is experienced, these are the qualities which provide the real creative achievement. There is a carry-over to writing, I'm sure. And these are not the inanities ever to be tested.

We need to recognize that writing is a venting. It is often, for that reason, therapeutic.

In Milwaukee County Children's Court, a 16-year-old girl was legally divorced from her parents; the parents initiated the action, citing what they felt was the inability to adjust to the girl's adolescent problems. She misbehaved and sobbed through much of the hearing. But the girl's probation officer introduced as evidence a poem the girl had written as she tried to express herself:

> Reach to touch
> yet only find space.
> Living to be wanted
> but not needed any place...

In Terezin and in Milwaukee the words were authentics. They recall words of another poet, Charles Doss, who said "A poem is often found in a spasm of anguish..."

And they may be found in very brief lines, chock full of imagery, the kind the prof celebrates in class. For instance, we all love that imagery of Carl Sandburg's where the fog comes in on little cat feet. Yet my own students have come up with brief imagery every bit as good. In 1979 Marianne Mongiardo's description of fog was this brief poem:

> Sky yawns at break of day
> and lets its morning breath give way.

Brief... and yet so effective! I think of that big sky yawning, sending out puffs of fog each time I encounter morning mist!

Sometimes the contributions come from non-writing exercises. A creative writing student noted in class that the Kraft Foods people were offering prizes for naming a new casserole. "We're supposed to be creative," Peg DeGraw said, "so why don't we try to come up with a name?"

Sounded fine to me. Then Sandi Towberman said, "I'll make the casserole and bring it to class. Then we'll have a better idea."

Nobody objected to that! And thus on Tuesday the classroom was the scene of a casserole feast. Frankly, I was not impressed with the dish, though it was carefully prepared and distributed. Some spaghetti, some meat, some green peppers, a few other ingredients. Not really novel. But it had the appeal for a large family -- everybody in on the act.

"What'll we call it?"

The names came quickly.

But then, after a half dozen peppered the brownboard, somebody captured the full appeal. "Come'n-Ghetti!"

And everybody knew that was the prize winner. The capturing of the mass appeal blended with the chief ingredient. What better name!

Kraft Foods apparently disagreed. But we felt very creative that day nonetheless.

The goals of creative writing courses are much more than prizes -- or income, or professional careers; they involve individual sense of achievement and expression. Whatever station in life, we all have access to those 650,000 words and the stories which we become aware of. James Fenimore Cooper had the right idea of individual achievement; in the early nineteenth century, after reading some short stories in periodicals of the day, he said to his wife, "Why, I could write better stories than these." His wife, even though not the writer, was the wiser of the two. "Then, why not go and do it?" He did -- and the classic Leatherstocking tales, our first authentic American frontier novels -- were born.

Sara was in my creative writing class; some six years later, now a housewife and mother, she wrote, "I think, with all respect to the post-adolescent poets in college, their education is not complete until they learn when to fail in meter. Creativity is lauded on campus; it's cute and even famous. Day dreaming is almost spiritual. We know what happens to old soldiers and bold pilots, but what happens to old daydreamers? There's no time, too much to do. No need to write, no assignment to fulfill. We can't all have delusions for sale."

Then Sara put the following in a block-letter paragraph:

"Do you know, old prof, what I do? I look out the kitchen window. I don't do what I should. I resent the imposition. I don't do what I can. Who needs it?"

Then, the heart of the letter:

"You once wrote in my journal that I was a creative person. If that's true, it's a curse and intelligence means perpetual purgatory..."

Is this the result of the prof's classes? Daydreams out of step with the world? Is creativity an abstraction without relevance to the household? Well, perhaps Sara's not truly creative. Maybe she's changed and lost that outlook. But then I read the next sentence -- and give her an "A" once again for expression:

"My neighbor is an avocado, but her kitchen is clean and her Spam and frozen peas are on time."

The "perpetual purgatory" Sara mentioned earlier does, in a way, symbolize the necessity of getting our words out, never blocking our minds. They're like runaways, pushing and shoving against the doors of our minds. And when I want to expand on that thought in class, I have my students ponder Richard Wilbur's poem "The Writer." He depicts the task of writing as that of a bird which seeks escape, having somehow gotten into an attic room of the Wilbur house.

One brief opening exists at the window; the bird tries and tries again to find its way out "Battering against the brilliance," dropping to the floor, "humped and bloodied," finally "clearing the sill of the world."

I want my students in creative writing to feel the emotion of being trapped, their thoughts trapped. I want them to batter and batter again, groping for the very best words and phrases, never content with cliches and vagueness. I cannot teach the experience of that effort, not give it to them. But I can develop their desire to want the freedom, and how to appreciate the best ways to achieve it. And I can discuss the outcome of whatever effort they have made.

I will never correct anybody into importance. But creativity does not come out of chaos. Frost said, "All that an artist needs is samples."

"Do you think you know all the answers about writing?" After class the question came, three of us in the room.

"If I did, do you think I'd be teaching here?" Still, you have to have confidence in yourself if you're to be a prof. Over the long string of years, I've received annual appeals from a professional education group to join that organization. Somehow, their appeals have never grabbed me. Particularly the one -- headlining their literature for a number of years -- which proclaimed, "Band together! Unless you join you will not get paid what you're worth!"

After a few of these, I sent a polite letter to the headquarters. "Of course I'm not paid what I'm worth," I explained. "I knew it would be that way when I chose a career in teaching. I'll never get paid what I'm worth! Do you think I'm so naive that I didn't realize that?"

The secretary of the group did not reply to my question.

Of course there are demands and problems -- and pay is always a factor. Many have sacrificed, and I'm sure there are inequities. But there is another element to the teaching game that can be a factor in individual thought about academia.

Sometimes we do not fully appreciate what we have until we have comparisons.

Small-college faculties are not for all persons; some may want the higher plaudits from wider audiences, some the mystique of larger classes, the sense of importance stemming from numbers alone.

And there is always the chance that some professors may feel the academics of the smaller schools are simply not as sophisticated, as "sound" as those of the vast university campuses.

The comparison, however, of most meaning came to me some years back when we had a gentleman on campus from one of the largest of the midwest universities. He was with us just for a day, giving a convocation program. However, some of us had the chance to chat informally with him. He gave the comparison most significant as far as I am concerned.

"How come you guys are this way? You seemed to be enjoying your luncheon together! And you talked openly about all sorts of departmental matters. How can you do that?"

Well, it was true -- we joked among ourselves, shared anecdotes about students, and about ourselves. I think we got a kick out of it. I tried to explain that to our visitor.

"Boy! That's not the way it is where I am!" He went on to explain that on his large university campus, departmental members simply do *not* talk to each other on any kind of a personal basis.

"Why?"

"We're all out to get above the next fellow. Everybody is trying to get that promotion, get that extra over the other fellow that might mean a bit more salary, a bit more recognition." He added that "you never share ideas -- they might help the other guy that way."

Mount Union College is no paradise for all, but in my 36 years of faculty status, I don't believe I ever encountered such a negative thought about my associates. It's almost automatic that the sharing is part of the job.

In the English department we had a steady seven members over most of those years. Yes, I can recall several personality clashes, but I do not recall any real bitterness, any avoidance of each other. Sure, there have been unusual circumstances on occasion -- I'm thinking of a departmental member many years ago who wrote poetry, taught poetry, but who had a personal frustration in that his wife was able to get more of her own poetry published than he had! Sometimes his frustrations showed in our discussions!

But overall, a basic respect for each other. Our departmental meetings were expressive of a common purpose. And when the vote was taken -- on any issue from a departmental requirement to a text adoption -- we all were supportive regardless of whether it had not been a unanimous vote.

Division? A don't-help-the-other-person philosophy?

Hardly. Perhaps the best response to that question would be to point to the "revolving" aspect of our department chairmen. The College moved to an approach where the department members -- in all departments -- would vote among themselves for the person to be the chairman of that department for a three-year period. Lower class load, more prestige went with the chair's status.

And a bit more work!

I can not recall any time when our seven members -- and the individual's names changed, of course, over the years -- had anything but an informal, supportive posture. Nobody ever "campaigned" for the chairmanship, nobody ever spoke out against any other person -- and we all chatted informally in our offices, the corridors, and in social gatherings on a light and supportive basis.

I'm not aware of anyone trying to "outdo" another in the department for fame, glory, status or position to dominate in any way.

Sure, there were some differences on occasion. Even a few split votes in our meetings! But we never held prejudice or animosity as a result.

As families we got together socially -- picnics, homes, special campus events and activities of "Campus Circle," the College's women's group -- close ties among us.

I believe most of us enjoyed the small college atmosphere.

And the comparison, so dramatically given by that prof from the large university from another midwestern state, brought it home to me.

Mount Union does have a lot going for it. And the faculty members are the ones who always have the opportunity to set the tone for both academic and social regard.

On any campus the prof is something more than a spectator, something less than a gang boss. Any serious student of writing should have at least two instructors. Not only is my own expertise and understanding just barely comfortable, but even if I knew more, my judgments would never be universally acceptable. We're dealing with art, not technicalities.

Maybe it's possible to teach the technicalities without the art; I doubt it, but I do know that one of the popular books on creative writing some years ago was titled *How To Write the Novel,* written by a husband and wife team -- who had never published a novel. Yet the text was apparently useful to many readers.

Kenneth Roberts, acclaimed for his many historical novels, said he was bothered by the would-be writers who, admiring their own letter-writing ability, expected to learn a formula, diet or routine which in a few hours time would convert them into best-selling authors. "Since I know of no such formula, diet or routine, " he said, "I must cease to talk to such persons."

How many have been conditioned by the bruising arm of "God?" Surely not the young man who, in a short story for me, said "He was struck in the right shoulder by an ice pick. Luckily it did not go through his heart." Or the young woman who created a character named "Cotton Smith" -- who got his name from his hair, "which was the color of wheat."

"God" thinks about those steps to the third floor of University Hall, the narrow office, the black pen and the steaming radiator. Emerson Sutcliffe's smiles the few times my writing pleased him. One time, many years after my graduation from Purdue, I had occasion to be on campus. Always sentimental, I walked the stairway again in that building, and found Prof. Sutcliffe still on duty. And of all wonders, he remembered my name. Again I took my place in the student chair, we chatted and I was eager to tell him about the publication I had achieved to that point -- my years as a trade journal correspondent, my published poems, my short stories which had found pages in several magazines.

"I knew you would do something, Mr. Crist," he smiled. What I had done, however little, meant something for him; it was authentic for me that moment, staging more circumstance out of the past. His voice a bit less strident, his face more lined now.

He looked out the miniature window as I tried to be as upright as possible in the straight-backed chair. I told him that my own office was relatively small, too. "I guess they figure profs don't need much room to keep prodding those young creative writing students."

When I left, he nodded slowly, then pointed out to me that Emily Dickinson had once written a poem which called attention to the fact that "the brain is wider than the sky."

And the campus may well embrace both.

15
English and the Technical World?

Christmas time at the local dime store. I was behind the counter during vacation, selling toy trains. Seventeen years old, I was a model airplane builder, average student in that junior year of high school, scared of girls, at home with the kids who came into the store to watch the 0-gauge trains run around in circles I made for them.

At counter edge, a five-inch glass partition lined the counter. Watching through it nearly every afternoon was a little fellow of eight or nine who stayed for hours, absorbed. His nose rested against the glass, winter's cold sending dribbles down inside the partition.

Most fascinating for him was the little signal tower I held; in the tower was a switch operated by movement of air. I'd hold the scale model tower to my mouth and give the orders: "Stop!" and the engine would halt. Then, after appropriate time, I'd say "Proceed!" The movement of air actuated the switch and the train resumed speed. I was king of the world, my commands part of a magical domain which held the little fellow in awe.

"Golly, mister," he said "You can control everything!"

Well, not quite. Watching this little fellow, my thought went back to another, younger than he, one who lived several blocks from our home, one who was pulled about by his mother, the youngster confined to a small wagon. He couldn't walk. I had serious physical problems at age six or so, but my parents had funds for the very best of care; and despite my use of crutches for quite a time, mother drove me to school every day, chauffeured me in style everywhere. But the

little wagon-boy did not attend school at all. Why didn't he have the same opportunities which came to me?
And why didn't I get to fly the airplanes of World War II? After Kresge's I devoured the air magazines, knew every part of the B-17s, the Mitchells, the Consolidated B-24s. I knew them only in imagination, and in the reading of manuals and magazines.
"Gear switch."
"Neutral."
"Turbos."
"Off."
"Brakes."
"Open."
"Trim tabs."
"Set."
The check list for the B-17. Later, I'd note that a cormorant is top heavy and awkward on soil, an eagle in cumbersome swagger, but aloft they are in brilliant beauty. Why did the other guys get to go off to war, fly the beauties, wear the uniforms, become the heroes? Just because I couldn't pass a physical, why did I remain on the sidelines, untouched by the daily drama in air?

I'd show them. If not a flier, I'd be a designer. I'd design the wings, plume the beauties, be part of the glory. Ignoring other signals showing interest in language, in communication more than in integral calculus, I went to Purdue's school of aeronautical engineering, spent lab times at the drawing board, studying Milliken's "Aerodynamics," conducting wind tunnel tests, wiring electrical equipment, calculating structural stresses, reading Eddington, Jeans, Einstein, von Karman. Getting a degree in aero engineering, staying on, teaching the Navy V-12 program, being part of the war effort (not so glorious now, for now I had known of the loss of friends).

The Purdue Alumni magazine in later years referred to me as "the world's most mixed-up English Professor -- or aeronautical engineer!"

Teaching writing within three years of graduation in engineering? Must have been a lousy engineer! It was the start of my second semester, junior year. My first opportunity to be able to take elective courses! Up till now it had all been requirement-requirement-requirement.

I was impressed with my new-found freedom and had elected a course in personnel management. Now, on opening day, I sat in the third row of the room staring blankly at the prof who had charts and diagrams regarding office management.

My enthusiasm waned quickly. Would other elective courses, within the engineering major framework, be no more intriguing than this? The prof droned, the office images he constructed were unimpressive. I squirmed. Never was a 50-minute session so long.

The large-university campus did have a heart, however. And, fortunately, a confused young man had the gumption to check it out.

I walked that January afternoon from the engineering complex to the area where the social sciences were concentrated. I was not thrilled, understand; the vision I had of psychologists was wildly gesticulating social misfits who paraded their own graphs, charts and diagrams to offer commentary on how to smile in public.

But I went to the departmental office, inquired about anything they might know to help.

"Is there such a thing as a test to find out what your interests really are?"

Though her name has faded from my memory, the warmth and aid the woman gave me that day -- and for a week of testing -- remains a tribute to the heart a large campus may have.

She took charge, gave a series of vocational interest tests which showed -- alas! -- that engineering was far down on the scale.

"You ought to be in something to do with writing," she said. "Or teaching." They ranked highest by far. Even sales was above engineering.

Now what do I do? I was already started in my second semester, junior year.

She took over, talked to the engineering school officials. I did my share, too. And a program was worked out whereby I would take a double minor in English while finishing my more-than-half-concluded aeronautical engineering degree.

I dropped the office management course. A week had passed, but I was allowed in an advanced writing course nonetheless. On my way!

Remaining with the engineering curricula, as well; I was in great demand during the senior lab courses.

Who would go through that nasty, sweaty task of writing up the lab reports, putting into words the results of the tests? I always volunteered. Everybody, as a result, wanted me to be on their team! And while others put in overtime to conduct extra-credit lab experiments, I spent my time writing scripts for the campus radio station and newspaper. A Navy V-12 classroom experience whetted my appetite for teaching, so it was on to graduate school at Indiana

University for a master's in journalism. I had a double minor in English at Purdue and with close cooperation of the two Indiana state schools my combination was feasible.

The move made sense; I couldn't see spending four years at a technical school just to find out what "x" equalled. Compounding problems was the fact that frequently when I did find out what "x" equalled, everybody else had a different answer!

The office of the mathematics department chairman at Indiana U. was a rambling affair; Dr.Thomas listened politely to my inquiry about part-time teaching. "One more time. Let me get this straight." His look was puzzled. He had his pipe. And tweeds. Every bit a prof. "You have a degree in aeronautical engineering, right?"

I confirmed this.

"Now, you are in graduate school here in Bloomington. In journalism." He waited for my acknowledgment.

"And you want to teach math this year?" He muttered something about "these changing times."

The assistantship went well. And I think I'm the better for this unorthodox background; a wide range of interests helps my appreciation of literature of all types. I am not, of course, the authority of most of my colleagues on British literary heritage. At a National Council of Teachers of English convention, the prof who would introduce me (I was giving a scholarly paper on teaching machines) was obviously bewildered as he looked over my biographical data. "Maybe the best thing," he confessed, "is just for me to ignore the whole thing. I don't think they would understand."

A hunter of "x" is not the type the literati readily accept!

I think of Lewis Carroll. *Alice in Wonderland* is full of linguistic by-plays -- an important consideration, recalling that he was a mathematician by trade. The King and Alice, in a scene, are waiting at roadside for the appearance of the White Knight. "Do you see him?" the King asks.

Alice replies, "I see nobody."

"Amazing! How can you do that?"

Later, when the White Knight appears -- having run the entire distance, now, puffing considerably -- the King bawls him out for being so late.

"I don't see how I'm late," the Knight argues. "I ran all the way. Nobody beat me here."

The King responds quickly, "I know -- and she saw him!"

E. A. Abbot dealt with a larger situation. Also a mathematician, a hunter of "x," Abbot created a hero perhaps prophetically named "A. Square." He's the central figure in a less-known but equally fascinating novel of the late 19th century titled *Flatland*. It's a two-dimensional world, one of width and length. Into Mr. Square's living room appears a three-dimensional sphere from a three-dimensional world. In answer to Mr. Square's question "Where did you come from?" the sphere replies, "Above."

"Above" is not in *Flatland* dictionaries. It has no meaning whatsoever. As the story continues, the sphere takes Mr. Square on a journey to "Lineland" -- a place where all creatures are of but one dimension, length, and whose lives consist merely of going back and forth in a single line. The sphere and A. Square boldly intrude, coming into Lineland. It has no meaning whatsoever.

Having learned that there is indeed a "side" and an "above" in the world, A. Square returns home, tries to tell his neighbors of the world beyond their experience. His language fails him; they conclude he is insane, and place him in an institution. Imagine! He thinks there is something called an "above!"

How stupid!

The book is A. Square's memoirs, written in secret in a padded cell, with hopes that some day someone in *Flatland* will read and consider -- and will lead his people out of the narrow vision which has so long dominated them.

I first read *Flatland* in the restricted, specialized mathematics library at Purdue. Integral calculus, Fourier series, trigonometric functions, and all the paraphernalia of advanced mathematical logic all around me -- and I would never have known of E. A. Abbot's very instructive tale, except for that engineering degree I wanted.

Today, seeing a report of the official British examination of several tragic crashes of one of their airliners, I find a report noting the cause as a "lack of integrity" of one of the airframe members. "Integrity" is in unusual juxtaposition, a philosophical term; yet its sense of "lack of wholeness" is appropriate. If a person is to be trusted six nights of the week but not the seventh, he lacks integrity, a wholeness or consistency. The airframe member carried its load most of the time, but under certain stress conditions it failed, lacking integrity. Perhaps the aeronautical engineer who wrote the final report is a bit of a philosopher, perhaps a linguist.

What role can words, poetic expressions and nuances, play in the life of anyone who is not an English prof? Do creative words have relevance for engineers, for all in technology?

The story is told that Duke University inaugurated a compulsory writing course for all engineering seniors, to make sure the technical graduates could express themselves adequately. Nobody in the senior class was pleased. "We took freshman comp," they wailed. "We're seniors. And who needs to know more about writing, anyway?"

Petulant, defiant, they filled the lecture hall wherein the ignominious course was to be taught. In strode the English prof, the hated one. He surveyed the class coldly -- then made a startling announcement.

"You don't want to take this class -- and I don't want to teach it. You're seniors. You had a writing class four years ago. You're technical people. I think this course is entirely unnecessary."

Stirrings! Beautiful! The class leaned forward in unison, smiles appearing at least. "Right on!" they intoned.

The prof continued. "I think we can all get out of this course."

"Great!" The volley rang throughout the hall.

"All we need to do is write a letter to the Dean of the Engineering School expressing our concerns, our reasons, and our conclusions."

"Huzzah!" Or the equivalent.

The prof was happy. "All right, now. We'll draft a letter. Who in here will volunteer to write the letter that will convince the Dean?"

Deafening silence.

"Isn't there anyone in here who can write this letter on our behalf?"

No response.

Then the prof dropped his smile. "My God, you're seniors and not one of you can write a simple letter of persuasion. We have no time to lose. Let's get down to business."

Then he added that the course would be "much more difficult" than he had originally planned.

Sometimes we have to get back to the basics!

They can link communication and science, of course. Reading Sir James Jeans, Millikan, Eddington or the science writers of more current times, you find the knowledge of science is enhanced through clear but at times poetic writing. After all, poetry emphasizes pictures and comparisons, analogies and metaphors. C. W. Ceram in archeology, Ernest Gann in aeronautics, Carl Sagan in physics bring the freshman English class right into their books.

There can be poetic forms in mathematics. Lillian and Leslie

Lieber explain that complex topic in free verse -- delightfully so -- in a book I came across many years ago, while still struggling with some mathematical explorations. *The Education of T.C. Mits* is the title -- the protagonist "The Celebrated Man In The Street."

Newspaper people can write with poetry too. I recall the in-depth article in a Sunday paper about the impact of certain chemicals -- sulphur dioxide -- upon the giant Washington monument. A chemical reaction occurs, albeit very slowly, over the years, slowly eroding the mammoth structure. The chemicals coming from industrial impurities now taking more and more hold on the atmosphere. Well, all of this made sense, but had little impact upon me -- until the science writer put it into an analogous situation.

"The Washington monument," he wrote, "is acting like a giant Alka-Seltzer ... you can almost hear it fizzing as you drive by!"

Now I get the picture!

The writing helps. So does the perspective.

In the 1920s a series of railroad track failures prompted the University of Illinois to establish an elaborate laboratory series of experiments to determine the cause. All types of railroad cars were brought in, impact tests were conducted, rolling stock again and again run over the tracks. The experiments ran for several years without conclusions as to why fissures appeared in the tracks. A graduate engineering student, going over the test results raised the question which ultimately solved everything. "Maybe it isn't the loads at all; has anybody thought about the way the tracks are fabricated?"

Impurities in the original operations, the extruding process were found responsible for the fissures. Years of tests had been focused on the wrong aspect of the problem.

We all need fresh views of our work. In recent years I've found that my seminars on creativity go over just as well (better, in fact) with corporate groups of engineers and technicians, than for groups of professional writers or writers-to-be. I cannot tell an engineer how to solve some mathematical, structural problem; I am a 10-year-old in awe of the magic tower controlling toy trains, in comparison. But the basics in creative problem-solving, creative expression, creative artistry apply to all, because they stem from the same mental chemistry that, in its own way, is involved with equations.

E. A. Abbot was not writing about irrelevant fantasy; putting one thing in terms of another, he was telling us about the blind spots we have -- and which can be overcome.

The blending of the technical with the humanities looms more and more significant. We have capabilities to manufacture horrendous devices of destruction, but the ethical surfaces -- perhaps more now than ever before -- to remind us of the inevitable partnership, man and mind. Einstein saw the blend. He wrote, "All science and technology and humanity conspire to liberate us..."

At least one English prof is satisfied that the science and technology are part of his academic pedigree.

The conspiracy was a good one.

16

It Never Ends

They will fade,
the names, blurring
with time's watershed, curling
the directory's pages.
One says, "Remember
the fellow with curly hair,
they called him 'Red,'
by the window?
And the girl with look intent?"
We live in cycles,
the campus geared to
annual courses, term projects,
commencement lines which
wind across the quad
in catalogued rhythm.
They will change the world,
some will become the leaders,
and still
unremembering, even one
(with curly red hair by window
or with look intent)
we know less of more.
I call the serialed names
from master lists in the

       blocked computer print
       and some will change the world.

       I begin the term
       knowing some will fade;
       I end the term as my lifetime spent,
       noting one with look intent,
       remembering what was said
       by one with curly hair of red.

One of the students caught in the trauma of 1970 was forced to leave our campus under a cloud. Nevertheless, our relationship has remained a good one. "I've tried to avoid goodbyes," he wrote just before he left.

"I've made the awesome discovery that even when one's whole life has consisted of relatively if not completely permanent goodbyes every few years, saying 'goodbye' to such a large chunk of one's life as I left here is still a very difficult thing."

In that note, written in much haste not so to avoid the wrath of faculty and administration but much more the judgment of some students who felt misused, Steve enclosed a poem from his father. A long statement, it depicted the enemy on the Ho Chi Minh trail, a specific soldier who was "a little browner, a little scrawnier, but not much -- the jungle makes us all scrawny..."

He found "his eyes containing a reflection of my own eyes." The poem noted:

       It may seem fantastic,
       but at that moment I was not sure
       which one of us was which
       and if each of us was either
       or both...

       I didn't know whether I was more afraid of him
       or of being confused --
       Confusion is a terrible fear.

And the poem concludes this way:

       So
       I killed him.

At least, I think it was him.

He was right; confusion is a terrible fear -- and sometimes we strike out at others; students making snap judgments, condemning faculty, and they, in turn, judging students on surface matters only.
We kill each other.
Or we think it is each other.
Or is it ourselves?
Steve wrote to me, "It is much easier to realize all these things removed from the heat (from fires or from big mouths) of involvement. You and I found some agreement even when we found ourselves peering between the rails of a fence at one another. At the time of involvement that can be a misfortune; in later time and place of neutrality, it is a joy."
And some day we will all learn that such joy stems from being willing to probe from a principled basis, not from emotion.
We may someday come to know whether we have killed our enemy or ourselves.
I'm glad Steve took the time to write. I remember him. There are others. Duane Rosenlieb, now successful in a professional career, had some troubles trying to find both academic proficiency and social harmony. He took the creative writing course as well as basic journalism, but found, perhaps, his best expression in a simple note he sent to me in time of personal crisis:
"I am probably the only person in the world," he wrote,"who bleeds through the point of a Flair felt-tip pen."
Others have bled, too, through their pens, placing words, sharing thoughts. I cherish the evidences of awareness. Back and forth through the flood of years the cameos of students come with insights.
Creative writing. 1965. He sat in the third row. A student in basic composition three years before, he was doing well -- and with cause. Ample talent, fine personality with pleasant shock of hair tumbling in easy laughter around his amiable face. His questions were not the most profound, but he was active, curious. His poetry showed fair promise.
Take the poem apart. Ask the questions. Why this word? Why not that word? What is meant here? Could it be this instead? And you get out some poems by John Ciardi, formerly of Rutgers, long time poetry editor at the *Saturday Review*. Ciardi is a hard nosed fellow, putting thoughts on line.

You bring Ciardi's *Elegy Just in Case* to class. You like the poem not only for its genuine theme, but for its example of hypothesis, of novel theme. He was a gunner in World War II. The poetry in him got the better of the gunner at times, and thus *Elegy* was written. A message to his family should he not return alive. In part, Ciardi wrote:

> Here lie Ciardi's pearly bones
> In their ripe organic mess.
> Jungle blown, his chromosomes
> Breed to a new address.
> Progenies of orchids seek
> The fracture's white spilled lymph.
> And his heart's red valve will leak
> Fountains for a protein nymph.
> Was it bullets or a wind
> Or a rip-cord fouled on Chance?
> Artifacts the natives find
> Decorate them when they dance.
> File the papers, pack the clothes,
> Send the coded word through air --
> "We regret and no one knows
> Where the Sgt. goes from here."

My purpose with the poem was elemental: "You can write poetry about any topic. Not just sunsets and forests and falling in love. See what John Ciardi has done, looking to the future and possible consequences. Work on a wide range of themes. Poems can be written about anything -- as Ciardi has shown us."

You make your point, then go over the reading assignment. The text mentions the role of honesty in writing this day; useful discussion follows. Some notations on the brownboard then, followed by brief reference to cadence in something Poe had written.

You dismiss class, meet again... and the years come and go like the new kids on campus, spilling down the hallways of your thought, the Septembers again, the brownboard notations, mention of Poe or Ciardi or Dickinson, and one day, in the bitterness of southeast Asia that raged all about us, but which had not really touched me, I read of the death of a young pilot, now a married man, now an alumnus with distinction in battle. At age 23 Ralph was returned to the States, he of amiable face and pleasant shock of hair, never to be seen again.

Weeks then into months and a letter comes to my office,

something from Ralph's mother. "We know he took creative writing from you," she writes," so I thought you might be interested."

There was a poem he had written "some time ago" to the family; something written while he was caught up in the Viet Nam War, a poem by this young man who learned of cadence and of honesty and of example.

I put down the letter, looked at the poem she had enclosed.

> I had a rendezvous with death
> Over this country so green
> with its towering mountains
> and picturesque scene.
> I gave my life so young
> to keep my country free
> after leaving my family and wife
> by crossing the big deep sea.
> Though since I died so far from home
> away from those I love,
> I pray that none will cry
> but remember the sign from above.
> That death is not final
> a mere slumber it will be
> until God awakes each dead man
> to live in eternity.

The office walls disappear, the day is of a time past, the communion now complete, the shock of hair tumbling throughout my mind, for I know what prompted him to take on this assignment for himself, to write yet another poem without thought of grade but only of the genuineness of message.

I pictured him writing, thinking of John Ciardi's poem from class, determining to write his own *Elegy -- Just in Case.*

Just then a young woman popped in the office, smiled, "Prof. Crist? Can I see you a minute? About the Fitzgerald paper..."

I did not respond for a few minutes; she probably thought it strange. But I was back in the classroom, talking to Ralph Hunt, Jr., the classroom where John Ciardi, too, was standing, nodding approval. We were together in a strange and beautiful time and as long as it lasted I did not know of the other student in the doorway.

"Mr. Crist? The Fitzgerald paper?"

They parade in my thought. Not names and numbers. But hearts and souls.

And from southern Ohio, from a very small high school, came Clarence, a freckled young man with a desire to preach the gospel -- but having a woeful inadequacy in written expression. Trying to be helpful -- we've made many mistakes in trying -- the admissions office accepted Clarence on a probationary status. The proposal was this: enroll in two summer school classes; if you pass both, you will be admitted as a full-time student in September.

There were just five others in the basic composition class. We pushed through grammar, rhetoric, literature. I had them keep journals, indicating these would not be graded as such, but that they would be helpful to the students in this basic composition class, reflecting their overall work.

Clarence did not make the grade. His work was not even close to passing -- all the misspellings, awkward sentences, inadequate punctuation, even the lack of effective ideas to deal with. At the end of the five-week summer term, I counseled him to approach the examination with extra caution.

"If you pass the final, you'll probably pass the course."

Ah! How easy for the prof to eyeball on that statement, put the hand on the shoulder, smile sagely, and then stride away.

I did not collect the personal journals. On examination day Clarence came in, read the assignment -- to develop a paper of response to Jacque Barzun's book *The House of the Intellect* which we had studied. Then he struggled through his assignment during the entire three-hour period allotted.

He turned in the paper, a bit nervous as he extended his hand to me. "I appreciate what you've done for me."

I knew he was sincere. "We'll see about the grade, Clarence. I'll do my best for you."

His turn to eyeball me now. It was direct, then he withdrew his hand, walked away. I did not want to grade the paper while he was there. The others had left some time before and I had glanced through theirs while Clarence labored. Now, in the quietness, I picked up all the papers, deciding to wait till evening at home for the grading. I noticed a small notebook under the desk chair where Clarence had taken the exam, picked it up to turn in to the lost-and-found file.

The exam was far below standard. I turned in the grade the next morning, never saw Clarence again. He had failed the history course as well and could not be admitted to Mount Union.

Absent-minded as always, I neglected to put the notebook in the file. Several weeks later, getting ready for the fall term, watching the incoming freshmen stroll around campus, their Sunday evening picnic to start the term, the laughter, friends being made, the edge of college around them. Time for another English 100 class. Well, I was ready. Our family trip to the west had been rewarding, the river and white water we experienced, the trails. Good to be back now, ideas stored up, experiences ready to he shared. Some students in Chapman Hall already, peeking into the rooms they would use the next day.

In the office, I pushed aside the mail, found the notebook still there since early August. Throw it away now? Let's see now, who was that kid? Might be his. It was well filled, entries of a personal nature -- more of a diary than a writer's journal. Might have his address in here.

The last page. "Mr. Crist says I must pass this final examination... It means everything. It means college. Oh, God! Be with me in this hour!"

That was decades ago. Clarence's notebook is still in my desk, a constant reminder, a constant goad, awareness.

We deal with souls, not faces.

Such as burly, towheaded Dave who argued his way through three of my classes. Who sat by the door, as though ready to escape. Dave who said a decade ago "How do you know how to grade my work?"

"As I do others' work. And you've missed several of the key assignments."

"Yeah, but I did the reading. And I did the discussion. Maybe I am not ready to do all the writing at this point."

"How shall I grade?"

"I dunno. You're in the driver's seat. You're the one playing God."

How many years later was it? Two? Three? They found him in a room in Cincinnati. His life span ended; too many drugs, too much in the arm. A classmate told me, "It's so sad. He had so much going for him."

Including a grade of "C" in creative writing. Not what he felt he deserved. Was there some relationship between my grade and his addiction?

I neither drink nor smoke. Never have. I'd love to have all my parade of students fall into that pattern for I know their lives would be so much more rewarding if they avoided the slavery of such habits. But I recall what Kahlil Gibran said -- "a teacher can take you to the threshold of his mind, but he does not conduct you thither-ward."

It was not my place, my post, to have students think exactly as I do. Nancy Ward phrased it this way in her writing class journal many years ago: "Mr. Crist has opened a door, but I'll have to walk in by myself."

We deal with lives. You cry and you laugh. You have the full spectrum. Because you're a prof.

You get reminders of these -- you need them -- all the time. Sometimes you revel in the malapropisms they come up with.

One fellow wrote, "My brother had his leg decapitated."

One girl wrote, "My grandmother always wore a turbine on her head."

I laugh -- and point out their errors. And somewhere back in my thought is the classic statement by George Saville to keep me in line. Writing his Maxims back in the 17th century, Saville, the first Marquess of Halifax, put it this way: "The vanity of teaching often tempteth a man to forget he is a blockhead." I needed that.

Blockhead or not, the prof affects many lives. Not just fun, games, classes, language. The prof is never quite sure how far the teachings go. College itself isn't going to make a big difference in anyone's life. I tell my students that more than grades and courses is their personality at the time of their job interviews. Their alertness, their liveliness. If the student draws any lessons beyond the textbook, then the example of the prof needs that same sense of life and exuberance. If the prof must take the stars of remembrance with him into the classroom cavern to create his own joy, so the student must as well to his campus situation, his career situation.

Some do not find it possible to remain on campus. "It seems inevitable now that I am amid problems at home, that I will have to abandon all hopes of continuing at Mount Union," Cathy wrote me. "Mr. Crist, it all seems so foolish! I actually believed that I could rise above my present situation and become somebody worthwhile. Now it seems I am destined to a life of waitressing -- and of scrounging for the extra money to purchase those little luxuries I may desire occasionally."

She had written a year after her freshman class with me. "I wish I had a million dollars, so I could give my family and others those necessities lacking. My parents drag themselves through the side door after a full day of toil, being sure to wedge a tattered cloth between the broken door latch and its frame so that it will not fly open..."

"I know that money cannot buy happiness, but sometimes I wonder if, indeed, money does pave the road, making the journey less troublesome. Now, more than ever, I realize why so many people turn to smoking, drinking and drugs as an escape from their ever present dilemma."

My reply was lengthy; in part as follows: "Consider something far worse than what you now experience: the poverty not of money, but of thought. The lack of ideas or perceptions. Money is a means of getting things, but how do we get the thoughts which always transcend mere things? Money cannot buy perception. We cultivate it, demonstrating by degrees what we have built into us... you have perceptions and purposes. You are a wealthy young woman."

The prof believes this. The prof wants her to see it. The prof hopes he has expressed it in the right way. The prof wonders if he knows how to write at all.

It will be mailed on the way home. First a stop in Beeghly Hall, the administration building. The Registrar will want the new set of grades, stop by to see the Dean of Women, make sure the chubby girl, front row, left, is feeling better now. Then to the alumni office, chat with the secretary at the main desk there; she's been here as long as you have. Then to the gym and watch the basketball team in practice. And there's Prof. Markley from the math department, gym bag in hand.

"Racquetball one of these times?" He's a good one.

You hear the sounds from the courts at the end of the building. Your locker in the faculty section is number 17 -- and you haven't used it for some time. "I'll be in touch!"

The oldest adage is the one which says that college professors do not die... they merely lose their faculties. The succession of meetings, committee discussions, sub-committee involvements and one-on-one debates (sometimes bordering on harangues) suggests that our faculties remain forever wedded. Until the late 1960s, our faculty meetings (monthly) were out of reach of the students. It isn't that we were anti-student, but tradition held. Oh, we weren't as snobbish as the European universities which had separate classroom doors for the good doctors -- and those good doctors were always deliberately 10 to 15 minutes late for class, just to give those kids a lesson as to who waits for whom! But not all things are changeless.

After the takeovers and concerns of the 1968-72 era, the faculty voted to have the Student Senate appoint two students who would be welcome at our sessions. For most of them through the years since then I doubt that any discussion has been more controversial than open dorm hours.

Well, more has been discussed, but much of it I cannot fathom unless I've been on all the sub-committee sessions. And by the time all those reports reach the full faculty, I was more weary of them than emotionally wrought.

There was, however, precedent for students coming into the faculty sessions prior to the actual admission of delegated ones. And I'm responsible. Partly.

The faculty was meeting in formal session in the Alumni Room at the campus center. A dignified, sober meeting with many academic matters discussed. A meeting that had not planned on the arrival of Georgia, a senior. She was an advisee of mine; a delightful, lively girl who had a boyfriend in another state. She had discussed with me many times her romance and the sometimes up-and-down pattern it had taken recently. I counseled, playing the role of advisor beyond the merely academic realm. Then one happy day Georgia announced all was well.

"He's going to marry me!"

Wonderful! And so it was a few days later I found myself in the dignified faculty meeting. I had no idea what chaos an indefinite pronoun would make at that meeting: The door at the rear of the Alumni Room opened sharply at 4:40 -- right in the midst of our session -- and I heard the woeful wail of a student.

"Where is he?" A colleague at the rear of the room tried to quiet her. This only added to the tension. The girl's tears were evident to all who had turned around to see what was causing the interruption. Looking for me, she cried out -- using the indefinite pronoun:

"Where is Mr. Crist? *He* says he won't marry me now!"

He? Me?

I rushed out to calm my advisee, get her out of the room!

But I think my attempt only made the implication of "he" seem even more devastating!

However, for her it and all worked out beautifully; they married and have two lovely children, prospering now in Texas.

But there are still one or two in the meeting that day who wonder just whom she had in mind with that indefinite pronoun in the emotional cry!

Who needs textbooks for examples?

And on more routine days there are always the remembrances. You try to recall where the car is parked. You think of Cathy and money and values and absent-mindedness. You know that the State of Ohio spends three times as much money on liquor as on education, and you remember when cigarettes were taboo in all the buildings and you say to yourself what does all this have to do with education?

Besides, you can't even locate the car. You keep making little discoveries about your own value system and the practicalities of life. Your textbook on writing was no best seller and you wonder why, but who said you had to write a book anyway? Values. And grades to be turned in. What should come first?

You think of the tragic circumstances of Nellie Zimmerman who for 19 years was kept in a home for the insane simply because no one realized she was deaf and blind. No one really tried to communicate with her and she had nothing to respond with. And then one day someone took her hand and manualed "Hi" to her, opening a new world.

Have I held enough hands?

Maybe the car is along Miller Avenue... I'll swing over that way. As I do, I think of Dick Kinney once again. My last conversation with him was in October 1979. He passed away three months later. I had told him -- through the Tellatouch machine, making Braille dots into his forefinger as I type out the letters of my message -- of the beautiful autumn we had experienced. I mentioned the foliage, the clear blue skies, and the russets and ambers of the leaves.

"Yes, I know it has been a beautiful autumn," he replied readily.

And then he added, "Wouldn't it be grand if everybody lived as though we really deserved it!"

Coming from anyone else, the sentiment would be upbeat and positive. But coming from a person who had not seen anything for 49 years at that point, and who had not heard anything for 36 years -- well, it will always carry that "extra" value.

And all who knew him were recipients of perhaps the best gift of all -- the personal example of achievement, the example that, if we all try as much, would uplift every one of us.

That's what all profs and students can do. In the degree we understand the great freedom to learn, to see the beauty.

We'll get to the very core of ourselves. That human heart and soul. Maybe I wasn't so far off after all, when I put that in the non-best-selling text.

Souls, not faces. Profs teach remembrances. Statistics and formulae take care of themselves. Profs can share remembrances.

You never know what you'll get into. In the last days of the final semester of my 36 years of teaching at Mount Union, I asked each member of my freshman English class (at Mount Union every prof teaches freshman English; we're all in it together!) to write down one specific question. "After all, professors know everything," I said, with a grin. I was curious; what would be a specific question at the top of a student's mind?

You keep on learning. Here are some that were given to me that awesome Wednesday in April 1989:

> Why should college grads get all the good jobs?
> Why are good men either taken, gay or dead?
> How is Christ related to Santa Claus?
> Why do we fall in love?
> How does a clock work to age us?
> How many licks does it take to get to the tootsie-roll
>   center of a tootsie-roll pop?
> How can people kill unborn babies?
> What color is God's skin?

Not one question about the essays we'd studied, the themes we'd written, the debates we'd had. But the prof added more to his remembrances!

Earlier that day someone had put a note on my office door: "It was a good course, prof, even if it is only worth a "C+" from you, which is terribly upsetting. After all, there was a lot of work there, even for this lazy kid!" Added to the typewritten note, an afterthought, written after the note was taped to the door, evidenced by the shaky lines:

"Who is this kid who comes to your office with such audacity? When will he learn to spel?"

I smile, thinking about Duane now. I am strangely alone walking to Miller Avenue, now moving in front of Chapman Hall. I think of that lazy kid. I could write a story about him. And all the others.

What was it Cathy had written? "...my parents drag themselves through the side door being sure to wedge the tattered cloth between the broken door latch and its frame so it will not fly open..." Specifics. Picture words. The stuff of communication. In their own words, Duane and Cathy are both poets.

Maybe that's what education is all about: discovering the poetry in all of us. And discovering, at last, where you had parked the car. You are glad you do not teach at a large university. You'd never be able to find your car! And too many students. You wouldn't get to know them.

How many students have I touched? How many have I reached out sufficiently to know, to help? To discover?

Discovering comes in so many ways. I think of an interview with Karen Gearrald at the Hadley School in Chicago, when I was researching for that book on Dick Kinney. Karen, born blind, was a fine poet as well as head of the English department there, a beautiful, radiant, lively young woman. We shared our poems, finding more than in the formal interview. When I left, she held out her hands.

I just wanted at that moment to show my regard for her in some way other than a mere handshake. I put my hands to her face, touched her cheeks. An old fellow doing such a thing!

Her hands instantly moved to mine. She held them tightly against mine, mine against her face. Then she said, "Now I know more about you than all of your poems could say!"

Communication. We discover the manifold ways. Remembrance of that single act had tempered the gusto with which I teach written poetry. And made me aware of the infinite modes of expression. For the 36 years that I held that post at Mount Union College there has been a panorama of mutual endeavor -- prof and students which has been invaluable.

The career has been rewarding in manifold ways; each encounter an opportunity to appreciate the real beauty of the campus -- not trees and buildings, but the hearts and souls of all the students.

I think back so many times to that letter I received from the reviewer of my text *Man Expressed* in 1971 -- exactly mid-way in my Mount Union College career.

I had begun the text of some 246 pages noting "Don't take writing lightly. It's the stuff of which we communicate to one another and testify to each other's heart and soul."

It had seemed too dramatic for one reviewer, the one who wrote, "The eagle was fun, but how in hell do you get all that crap about the heart and soul?"

How? Because that's what writing is all about. And now, after 36 years of teaching at Mount Union College, I know it applies to the classroom as well.

Teaching is also always about the heart and soul.

Like, it really is.
You know what I mean?

Acknowledgements

"Elegy Just in Case" by John Ciardi from *As If*, Rutgers University Press, 1955.
"The Garden" from *I Never Saw Another Butterfly*, McGraw-Hill from State Jewish Museum, Prague, 1962.
Ben Franklin petition from *Gobbledook Has Got To Go*, U.S. Government Printing Office.
Flatland by E.A. Abbott in *The World of Mathematics, Vol. 4,* Simon & Schuster, 1956.
Lines of "Chapter One" by E.F. Benson in *Books and Bipeds*, Vincent Starrett, Argus Books, 1947.
"Out of Chaos" from *Harp of Silence* by Richard Kinney, Parthenon Publishing Co., 1967.
Lines from "Spring and Fall" by Gerhard Manley Hopkins from *Norton Anthology of Modern Poetry*, 1973.
Hilbert anecdote from *The Wind and Beyond,* by Theodore von Karman, Little, Brown, 1967.
Kinship with All Life, by Allen Boone, Harper & Row, 1954.
Turn Not Paled, Beloved Snail, by Jacqueline Jackson, Little, Brown, 1974.
The Awakened Eye, by Ross Parameter, Wesleyan University, 1968.
Life on the Mississippi, by Mark Twain, P.F. Collier Co., 1875.

About the Author

Lyle Crist's years as a professor of English and Journalism at Mount Union College began in 1953.

Prior to that time he had served as a teacher for three years at Alliance High School, an instructor in writing at Iowa State College, an assistant in mathematics at Indiana University and a graduate assistant at Purdue University. His degrees are from Purdue and Indiana.

During his years at Mount Union he has served on various committees. He was also an advisor for the *Dynamo*, the College's student newspaper, and the *Calliope*, the campus literary magazine.

Crist is a native of Alliance, Ohio. His other books include *Man Expressed*, a basic freshman writing text; *Writing Creatively*, a text for creative writing classes; two collections of his poetry, *Runaways* and *Risking and Running*; and *Through the Rain and Rainbow*, a biography of deaf-blind Richard Kinney, who graduated from Mount Union in 1953.

Crist received the College's Great Teacher Award in 1967. He retired from Mount Union College in July, 1989.